SPELLBOUND

A Memoir

PJ Karr, Ph.D.

Archway Publishing books may be ordered through booksellers or by contacting:

Archway Publishing
1663 Liberty Drive
Bloomington, IN 47403
www.archwaypublishing.com
1 (888) 242-5904

ISBN: 978-1-4808-7945-4 (sc)
ISBN: 978-1-4808-7946-1 (e)

Library of Congress Control Number: 2019907029

Print information available on the last page.

Archway Publishing rev. date: 6/26/2019

Table of Contents

Dedication

Especially for Madre—

For being an independent, compelling, witty, and avant-garde woman ahead of your time...

For forsaking all your beaus and suitors to marry our treasured Dad, your authentic and forever love—John, Johnny, JJ...

For making a conscious choice to become a formidable, resolute woman who paved the state-of-the-art pathways. You valued intention and free will—quite different from your mother's journey. Your three, gratified daughters experienced the untold opportunities plus an attitude and propensity for healthy, impassioned outlooks on life *and* attentive, mindful living...

For electing to be a truth-seeking, undaunted, and visionary woman throughout your marital challenges and bliss—an amazing whirlwind, just shy of seventy-four, soul-filled years...

For being my lifetime role model who depicted the fine art of dialogue, the value of forgiveness, and the power of prevailing, unconditional love...

For your moxie to triumph as my priceless keepsake, after living fully—an authentic, stirring, and sought-after life of 97 years young...

Especially for JJ—

For electing to become an uncommon, masculine-feminine persona—a rarity for your generation of men…

For the mutual decision and love to "create" me, your last born child—a realistic debate with the health considerations for Madre. I am grateful that courage, unconditional love, and undoubtedly, the guardian angels reigned supreme…

For being a male role model who depicted the art of nurturing, the dedication to fatherhood, no matter how busy "life" became, and the unflappable supporter of my unique endeavors, pitfalls, and triumphant glories…

For joining your treasured wife and our superlative Madre to manifest a home and a world of opportunity—deliberate intentions to savor the positive moments, the leaps of faith, and a "release" of any negative energy or karma…

For the unforeseen power to remain my priceless keepsake, especially throughout your thirteen-year dementia and Alzheimer's saga. I shall always believe that the "mystique of JJ" and "knowing PJ's kindred spirit" were an *amazing grace*…

For your forever-feisty spirit and invaluable gift of JJ— my devoted Dad and smashing, colorful, and high-minded friend who stretched to reach 96 years young…

Acknowledgments

Heartfelt gratitude and praise, first and foremost, are sent telepathically and spiritually to my celestial, angelic parents. Beyond my dedication, a profound thank you for being my far-sighted, gifted, and loving-kind Madre and JJ.

Both of you envisioned, began, and savored the ingenuity to script and continue the family letters. This "Karr tradition" of creative letter writing became a tithe beyond measure.

Each of your daughters elected to honor and pursue the Karr tradition. If Patti Jo were alive, she would be penning her exposes. At this time of my life, I remain smitten and beholden to both of you.

I anticipate and cherish the composition of our yearly birthday letters, Beej. A few years ago, you spoke in an unquestionable, bona fide manner. "We are the only ones that chose to continue and write the birthday letters. We are the *last* ones…"

I accredit and value dearly—that each of us made a *conscious* choice to embellish the revered "Karr tradition." I am bold or bodacious PJ, deeming that we deserve a definitive, vintage bravissima—for our authentic sister-love and paying forward these intangible riches.

I have been awakened to the reality that this book pursuit, the "core" of writing a family memoir, remains a mystical, compelling, and humbling process. I acknowledge that the essence of the excerpts and my reflections are indeed *"the best of my recollections…"* about beloved Madre and JJ.

There are moments when I invoke my earthly wish. I conjure a PJ dreamscape of my parents jet-setting back. Doting upon Madre and JJ—for a few seconds, hours, a week, or a month—would indeed be the pristine acknowledgment.

Somewhere in that gift of time, I could exhume and spotlight the untapped sagas that enfold a family memoir. My accompanying "I *really* don't recall" expression in any chapter would evolve into "aha" moments. Possibly…

These wishful moments reappeared naturally, but replaced all of my aforementioned dreamscape. Instead, the daily writings emerged with my parents' angelic guidance—what to share with a world in need of unconditional love *and* what to honor as their private, intimate memoir.

I acknowledge that my clairvoyant parents would want me to reflect, write, and not aim for perfection. It was never a surprise. My own phrases of "imperfect perfections" and "tango on" came full circle.

I am compelled to endorse the other noteworthy, allied spirits. They witnessed the fearless, enterprising endeavors to stretch my boundaries of writing and unconventional quests.

It came as no great surprise why I wanted to acknowledge and applaud these valiant writers. They were the shepherding, ushering, and radiant beings at my prose, poetry, and storytelling venues.

These exceptional humans embodied and showcased the efficacy of unequivocal love. Their appreciative wit, virtue, and value of individuals who composted and dared to present their compositions, in-progress or polished to the hilt, were the real deal.

My confidantes were a manifestation of the ultimate goodness in our world. Namaste…

Introduction

Creative nonfiction and prose were welcome pursuits from an early age—at home, at school, outdoors, or through scribbles in the moment—wherever that phenomenon happened. By junior high school, as I read short stories or novels, the delights of writing fiction emerged. I never imagined that the genre of "memoir" would become another enlightenment of glorious, untapped abundance.

While pursuing college degrees and my professional pilgrimage, odyssey, and wayfaring, I delved into the evolution of my stories. I scribbled, scrawled, and stuffed my collection into file folders—the manila ones. At different junctures, I sent most of the tales, dramas, or comedies to diverse magazines.

Later, I created documents—the techno folders—with my epic journey. In 2017, one of my techno folders became a fiction book devoted to short stories and flash fiction. The namesake became *Cliffhangers: Dramas and The Renaissance*.

My pathfinding was not about to end. Was it happenstance? Serendipity? Was it my mother's intention to nudge me towards another realm? Maybe it was a precious enlightenment that emerges when writing a family memoir. Hmm…

I remember *where* my Mom stated her heartfelt decision. "PJ—take my manila-clasped folders from the nursing home. You *keep* them."

I half-smiled, glanced at her, and put them back in her nightstand drawer. She gave me that inevitable sign—her Madre look—with a raised eyebrow to boot.

We had read together in her nursing home that cold, windy afternoon of 2012, but mainly from the family treasure trove. These literary books rested gracefully on my parents' old maple bookcases that decorated her room.

Other weeks, we read the internet excerpts from my feisty, sister-friend, Arlene. I would share Arlene's photos and cache of gems from my iPhone, a fascinating and still-mystical device to my mother.

We always composed a grateful reply on the same day. Madre adored the "whooshing sound" of our email, jetting into the cyberspace to sweet Arlene.

Whenever an unexpected moment came—sharing what was inside those manila-clasped folders—my mother was never quite ready to read them together. Madre would pause with her "far-away" look. I finally knew why…

Madre affirmed, "We will read when you come another day. I know. They are Dad's love letters—anniversaries and birthdays. I remember *all* of them."

"Don't you want to read a few of them together? Maybe today?" I offered in a gentle cadence.

Madre shook her head. "Another day. Thank *you* for asking," she murmured softly, her voice trailing off as she patted my hand.

Another year slipped by…2013. My Dad had died two years earlier. Madre chose her words fervently that day, looking into the depths of my eyes. I had just murmured, "The eyes are windows to the soul—my soul that you know so well, Madre."

She reached for my hand and squeezed it gently. "Now—take the manila-clasped folders with you," Madre stated, pointing to her nightstand. "You read our love letters—for *your* book writing. You were an admired professor and published so much throughout your career. Now, I reread your new, creative books with photography. I am so proud. You will *always* love writing…"

Madre motioned to the nightstand again. "Take the folders with our love letters for *your* writing. You already know how to write and what to share with people—what the world needs now. Love sweet love…"

Our eyes brimmed with tears as I paused to massage her soft, petite hand. "Thank you, Madre," I whispered, gently raising her hand for an affectionate, reverent kiss.

It was summer, two weeks after her ninety-seventh birthday and just shy of two years after my Dad's death. My dear Madre and best-ever friend wanted to join her endearing soulmate—John, Johnny, JJ.

Madre made her divine sojourn. I believed that their interlocking souls began a unique journey, celestial and ethereal this time.

Fast forward—to 2016. I had been working on my infamous de-cluttering of closets, drawers, and storage bags. I was rummaging around, getting bored, and paused for a break.

There were the manila-clasped folders, stored for at least three years, near my suede and leather boots at the back of my bedroom closet. I glanced at the folders whenever I grabbed a pair of leather boots. I had not forgotten Madre's voice and loving messages. Each time, I made a choice—not to open the manila-clasped folders.

That evening on August 30, 2017 at 11:30 p.m., there were Madre's telepathic and heartfelt messages of "it is *time*…" In my comforting lavender, plum blossom, and pewter bedroom, I laid down upon my beckoning bed.

I paused. I began with three—deep, elongated, and purposeful breaths.

It was no coincidence. Just like my esteemed Madre, I had taken a few years to come to this moment. I finally began to read and became immersed…

World War II Letters

I pulled out a manila-clasped folder from the back of my closet. I yearned to pore over the power of their written words. My eyes brimmed with sentimental tears.

Here at my fingertips was their dawn, a genesis of the spell-bound tradition. It was 1945—another time and place. The loving-kind woman, my prized mother to be, had penned a unique letter...

Dearest John— It is January 1, 1945.

I've enclosed a sparkling, wedding-band card with an *envisioned* letter from our young daughter...

The man, my wondrous father-to-be, was in his early twenties and serving in World War II. Nostalgic memories of my mother telling me that my Dad wrote affectionate letters to my oldest sister popped up. Yet, I never knew that Madre composed the return letters, whimsical and loving words, that she envisioned Patti would write...

My oldest sister was a young child who only saw "her Daddy" in his Navy picture each night. Kissing his photo, they would include "Daddy" in their night time prayers. Madre's envisioned letter from Patti stole my heart...

Dearest Daddy, I can put my arms around Mummy's neck and say, "Happy Anniversary" and write you. I love you, wonderful father...

Already, I'm almost two and awful, awful proud of you…

Sending you kisses and hugs. Can you hear me laugh, Daddy, as you tickle me? I say and beg for more…

I'll never stop loving you—always be your "first little girl" even 18 years from now. Wait and see…

Next to Mum, can I be your second best girl—please? Gee! Thanks…

Here's a lot of sticky kisses and big bear hugs… I love you—Patricia Joan

Then this woman, my mother and best friend-to-be, continued her ultimate quest. John, Johnny, JJ—this Anniversary sweetheart letter was sent while he served in the war…

I am gazing at our gay and colorful tree tonight as I pen this…

How wonderful and precious life is here in America, still a free country. Granted, we all know sadness and heartache, yet we have a freedom few countries possess today…

You know—my beloved—every year as I write you our "special" letter, I feel happier than the year before. One more year of memories…

I realize that this coming year may be the worst we have yet faced, for our separation may really last a whole year …

Time will be endless….we can take heart and be brave…know ours is the sort of love that is enduring and everlasting, come what may…

I liked the verse on your card—I love you with all of my heart and I can never repeat it enough…

This is a year of separation and a test—I can still find peace within…

I remain secure in your love for me and mine for you…

I shall mold the character of our child… She'll never go to bed once without you on her mind…

Oh darling, I know the time will be even longer for you—out there somewhere…

I recalled my parents expressing how the World War II letters to each other were censored. My Dad wrote in their "secret code" so that

Mom would know his whereabouts. Dad wanted her to feel reassured, beyond the horrors of war depicted and portrayed in the daily news. She consoled him—with her devout letters...

When you get that "all alone" feeling, think of Pat and I, look at our pictures, and hear me whisper from my picture with that half-hidden smile...

I'm waiting for you, dearest John. I'll wait forever...

And, some of that awful loneliness will disappear—try it!

Winding paths, censoring, and secret codes...
War images and unremitting imprints...
Harboring their devout moments of love and hope...

During these times of turmoil and chaos, my Dad was involved in a lot of action. Later, when I was in elementary school, my mother relayed something else. Her best gift? That her love—John, Johnny, JJ—returned home alive. Her other blessing was that my Uncle Pete came home as well...

Sweet, handsome Joe was Nana and Grandpa's last-born son who yearned to be a fighter pilot. He volunteered to head out to the war, not pursuing his dream of studying to become a doctor...

Sadly, Joe never made it back home. His fighter plane was shot down at sea. I treasured my two keepsakes—the copper mug given to my parents and the stunning Navy photo of the Uncle Joe that I would never meet...

As I pressed onward to read, a multitude of Madre's letters evoked the utmost pride in me. Without any doubts or bias, my genuine admiration for this woman was blossoming...

My heart swells with pride. You are following our ideals, something we can one day instill in our children. We will have plenty of examples to set before them…

The oneness of our love will be the most convincing factor for our children…

We have much to be grateful for…

Pat was born on January 4th and you have always called her our "Anniversary child" and she is! One day we will all know peace…

I'd like to shout it to the whole world—maybe my eyes do tell everyone—I'm in love, madly in love…

It was January 1, 1948. How special—her John, Johnny, JJ—had returned home safely. Later, there was something else...

My Dad's other loss was sobering. More than half his Dartmouth classmates—250 to be exact—never came back from World War II...

Much later, at 19 years old, I was eager to pursue a collegiate pathway. I chose my internship purposefully. It was with men who returned from the Vietnam War—men who were unaccepted, yelled at, unloved, and criticized. Even women, usually nurses on the front line, suffered the post-traumatic stressors...

I conveyed the truth to my parents. "I would have been a conscientious objector with my generation's awful Vietnam War..."

My Dad looked at me. Then he spoke very softly. "No war is worth it. And, we felt like we had more purpose—a better economy and future welfare—serving in World War II. Your mother and I were damn lucky to be reunited..."

While I was typing this chapter in a just-write momentum, my "PJ signs" breezed in, dropping an undeniable heart anchor. My computer recharge topped off at 100 percent in the exact moment as my "look left..." sign. There it was—the highlighted, blue page 126...

Wow, 126—that was the age my Dad aspired to be. JJ told ALL of us repeatedly. Incredible—my ethereal signs since their deaths in 2011 and 2013 kept appearing...

Flashbacks—images and encouragements—came as well. There was a spitting image of that afternoon in her nursing home. Madre had given me the manila-clasped folders, speaking in a gentle cadence. Her encouragements came full circle—you are already a published writer, you will know what and when to share what the world needs now—love sweet love. It was time. I was compelled to compose...

I paused to reminisce about the adult-children I knew and familial stories—their oral history. They were privy, but never recorded or *asked more questions. In that moment, I felt privileged. A companion of my Dad wrote to my mother about the disquieting times of the war...*

This letter from Lt. George arrived from the Philippine Islands. His mother knew Madre. Lt. George knew my Dad. No further information, but the occasional letter that I found in the manila-clasped folders was riveting, sending chills through the core of my being...

It is December 14, 1944. It has been some time since I've written to you...

I'll see what I can do about getting a few lines written tonight. Of course, my success wholly depends on Tojo—usually comes over about this time and causes us to put out our lights...

I last wrote a V-letter, so I couldn't have said much...

You know we are in the Philippines. We were attacked when we came into land, saw a Jap plane shot down that same day...

There was just one night—December 6th—when the paratroopers landed. We could see the tracers off in the distance like gigantic fireworks...

It was fun for awhile and then a Jap plane got near us. We hit the foxholes but quick. They shot him down though...

Since that night all we have had—alerts, more alerts. You people know as much, if not more about what is going on over here than we do...

As I reread Lt. George's vivid descriptions, the chills and heart tugs arrived. What was Madre feeling in her heart after his undisguised letter? Whatever the family, friends, and Madre heard on the news must have been hellish, even surreal—but, very disquieting...

It was February 12, 1945. Madre was on her writing mission to JJ, expounding on his cold and hoping that he felt better...

I am having difficulty on taking pics (wow—120). The ones of Patty came out wearing her dresses in the kitchen...

Pat stayed at your parents' house for supper and listened to "The Shadow" with your Dad. He *really* thinks the world of her now. She is talking so much more than when you were home on leave…

She tries so hard to say long sentences. Tonight, she asked me if you were coming (on leave) to see me—a new way to find out if you'd come…

I told her, "Pretty soon." You don't know how I worry that you'll get shipped out into a hot climate and have those fainting spells…

Oh darling beloved, take care of yourself—for Patty and I need you terribly…

Wouldn't believe the cost of clothes—tan leggings, coat, and bonnet are $26. Isn't that awful for children's clothing? It'll fit her next winter, too….

About the family. I really can't say I have any awkward moments with your folks now. I just seem to fit! The girls will, even of their own accord, hold my hand when walking and display affection. I feel they are my sisters and I sure am glad…

Bridget and I are going to make your Dad a birthday cake. She told me the other day that she didn't know there could be such fun in simple things until I came into the family…

Life is funny, eh? I tried so hard and now it seems as though I didn't even have to work for it at all. It just came natural and everything clicks….

Aunt Mary had to go in hospital and she told me there was a wounded soldier at end of hall in the hospital that use to scream at night—hours upon end—that the Germans were going to get him…

Aunt Mary realized she was so well off, said it made your blood curdle just to listen and, he was at the far end of the hospital…

Oh John, I hope you don't have to go out and if you do, I'll nurse you back to normal life again with every ounce of strength I have…

Our little Pat tells me, "I'm pretty or cute" and it makes me feel wonderful…

It is as though the little tyke is trying to take your place, my dearest. Patty Jo sends peppermint stick and lolly pop kisses—they are sticky ones…

Undoubtedly, Madre adored penning the letters to JJ. They characterized the family celebrations at home, but conveyed the ultimate consolation—JJ's timely reunion. It was April 26, 1945...

I am glad I made a cake for your Dad. It was a huge success! He was surprised and tickled. He followed me to the carriage with Pat. "Thank you for cake and for candles on it…"

…you should have seen his face. Pat danced around. Gee, honey, I thought he was going to cry. He was deeply moved. Guess it's the first one he ever had. Pat said, "Oh, my! What a naughty boy Grandpa was to blow out the candles!" And, how he laughed…

This occasion lacks you and Pete at home, but we'll one day be a happy family again. If I keep these birthdays going, it'll bring us that much closer…

The one consolation we have sweetheart—that it's definitely a winning war we're fighting and we'll be reunited soon…

The war news is good, but evidently fighting until real peace is our motive…

Commanders don't want to shove our boys into some of those pocket traps, for that would be like mass slaughter to our own boys…

Although hard, it is best to wait a bit longer and see if lives can be spared. Our losses have been plenty heavy enough…

JJ had written about a week earlier. It was August 14, 1945. The mail was censored or delayed, contributing to their candid writings about hopes, dreams, and optimism amidst the war transgressions …

My dearest sweetheart: I received a nice letter from you today—it made me very happy. You bet we'll be together in the very near future…

The present set up will be radically revised, once the wheels of demobilization machinery START to roll…

The government has to approach gradually to retain its strength as well as releasing men. We are losing men off this craft for various reasons…

K— is at the hospital ship for his feet. Today, we lost another man with ulcers…

Our esteemed electrician is being transferred to another vessel. The sooner things are adjusted, the better we will be. And, the sooner we'll head for home…

As for letter writing—honey—time is limited. Though I would like to write everyone, it can't be done. That's why you're bearing my own burdens…

Say darling, will you do me a favor and find out details of government business loans? I'll give you specific banks…

Love to you, Pat, and the family. Always, Johnny

Demobilization was an understatement. There were titanic transitions in store for my parents throughout 1945. Madre was living at their Elm Street abode in Ludlow, Massachusetts. No mystery why she wrote boldly—that January 1st on their Anniversary…

Dearest heart of mine: I hope you are dreaming and thinking of me constantly…

…dearest you made me very happy by your reply to my wire—and then, this morning, I received your special delivery. I'm amazed that Ludlow would deliver on a holiday…

Oh, my darling I can't tell you how complete my happiness was to receive word you were *okay* and then to get your "special" letter…

I take it from the postscript that you are still in the hospital. Darling, take care of yourself, for you are my most treasured possession…

Without you, my life would be snuffed out as a candle…

You know, too, that these are not mere words—that our love is that strong…

This year, our sixth anniversary, is our happiest even though we are separated. Our love child is here with us…

Patti Jo was close enough to be our anniversary child. Her birth on January 4th was all we needed to round out our full life—it is a full one, right to the brim…

It's the beginning of a new year, one that should see decisive battles in this war. We are certain to lead to Victory, your return to the haven of my arms and home…

I wonder if you realize how happy I shall be at that time, just bubbling over with a fountain of youth…

Our 6th is the happiest, as the month of December was memorable. It taught me life—my niche in it—and at long last, it freed me of that "vague mother complex" that I have been tormented by, given my childhood…

Thank you for your patience and letting me find myself…

You were silent. Little Marge found out for herself. I feel you today—spiritually by my side…

You always want to take care of me—makes a deep, delicious ache within my heart…

I feel this year that I am really a woman. I notice the change when I give my love, so mature. This past year of being a mother has greatly filled me with wisdom…

I've told you before. I derive more pleasure from our yearly birthday and anniversary letters than I can express in words…

I'd like to make a suggestion. Why don't we carry it out each year of Patty's birthday and each succeeding child? You can write one and I'll do likewise…

The first years, they'll have to be saved. But, I am sure that idea, if carried out, should bring a unity in later years between ourselves and our children…

Each year, we can tell them of their development and what we've observed by writing a simple letter that comes from the bottom of the heart…

I thought your Christmas letter to Patty such a lovely one, my dearest. Aren't you glad now that we always wrote our yearly letter? You can readily see if you were to send expensive flowers but no letter how great my disappointment would be…

Ours is a love so great that we don't need those "extra" touches. We just need one another. Before I close…

I wish you a very Happy New Year, darling! I did on a telegram yesterday, but it was cut out (not allowed)…

May this year see the end of this war in which you, my dear, are doing your utmost to aid our country…

I am prouder of you this year in uniform, John—for you being in there only strengthens my ideals and yours in life. America is still a wonderful country and we are indeed fortunate that it's ours and that our children will one day claim it…

Their Dad is in there striving and enduring sacrifices so that we at home may know peace, order, and comfort…

Never for one second do I forget why you are in there, John. My heart bursts with love and pride. I am so glad I am your wife…

I'd marry you again and again, every day of the week. I know you'd do the same…

I almost missed something. I put this letter back in the envelope addressed: John Karr, SK2/C, 56th Construction Battalion, Co. D, Platoon 1. I saw a small, folded newsprint. THE RHYME BOX and prose were entitled, "Your Letters"…

I especially like this! Yours forever, Marge…

Whenever I feel lonely
Or the least bit blue,
All I do is take your letters
And read them through and through

They're full of inspiration,
Inspiration that can never die,
For when I think of you, my dear,
It makes the hours fly.

They wrap me up in dreams,
In dreams of you, my dear,
For with you at my side
I'll ne'er have a thing to fear.

They're beautiful and glorious

As beautiful as can be.

They tell me what I long to hear,

That you, my dear, love me.

What my letters do to you

Or put into your mind

I do not know, but I would write much more,

If only the words I'd find.

Again, I say I love you

Love you with all my heart;

For intense and bright as fire,

So nothing can make us part.

As I made headway with these World War II letters, there were surges of euphoric intoxication. My parents upheld one another in scripted words. They managed to cast a lustrous, shining light over whatever "ebb and flow" of darkness had recurred on their horizon...

As I was reading the next letter, penned on May 1st, I felt a reverberation. The hallmarks in this war—the deeper abyss—also created a different space for the soul-filled spirit...

For my parents, World War II became four years of moratoriums, holding patterns, disquiet, and anxiety. There was a tempering and revamping with the seasons—a tempo of hope and promise prevailed for my parents...

Dearest darling— It's rainy here again today. Gloomy weather...

However—war news sounds far from gloomy, as though peace announcement may come today…

I know I'm going to cry tears of joy once it comes thru—and greater tears the day Japan crumbles…

It seems the surrender of Germany may make the Japs get even shakier, don't you agree, darling…

Well, you should see our gay, young daughter's eye today. It's purple, blue, and swollen. Looks as though she might be fighting a war…

We will be mailing your Father's Day gift tomorrow. Would be funny if you got it as soon as Mother's Day. Now, aren't you all guesses and a gog…

Gee, I got your wonderful love letter of April 25th—made me happy, pepped up, and I've reread your words of love…

I've watched a love movie—Greer Garson and Walter Pidgeon. How marvelous…

In your letters, you can't repeat enough how much home, Pat, and I mean to you since your departure. It pleases, makes me happier than mere words can tell you…

Ernie Pyle's books set me to thinking of the war. He stressed the fact that home meant everything to men out there in wartime. He said partings were hard at first then easier as time went by, for time takes care of things just as in death…

I agree that wounds heal, just as yours has *somewhat* about Joe with time…

Dad's brother—Joe—was the youngest in their family of five siblings. Dad and my Uncle Pete saw plenty of action in their assignments, but returned home…

Joe died, his fighter jet being shot down and lost at sea. Later, my parents released his brave spirit by gifting his copper mug to me when I lived in Texas. Joe gave the copper mug to my parents—the first to know where they met, danced, and loved at first sight. And then—that they married secretly before Nana and Grandpa knew…

I was smitten with the poignant, indulgent stories of Dad's youngest brother. He set an ambitious goal to become a fine doctor. He was a "peach of a guy" to everyone that he met. Joe was a tender man who idolized that Madre and JJ became "lovers at first sight—that dance near Hanover..."

Both of my parents, even at the latter stages of their life, disclosed stories of Joe, tears welling in their eyes. Today, I paused to caress his copper mug placed purposefully in my kitchen. I saw and used it daily...

The fog, intrepid with vapors of obscurity...

Undaunted circadian rhythms of an ocean's abyss...

The seamist burial of a brave and kind soul, Joe...

An acquaintance reaffirmed my truths. "Bring out the fine china, the valuables. Use them! Don't store them. And, remember their beauty!" I am trying my best, Uncle Joe...

I smiled. An inner peace was hanging around as I reflected aloud. Uncle Joe—I am a loving-kind, fun, and free spirit that I believe you would fancy and dote upon, given your affinity for Mom and Dad...

My wish—to know and play with YOU on the other side. Right now? I am watching over your esteemed copper mug...

I returned to Madre's letter of promise—never forgetting their capacity for unconditional love and their transcendence throughout the perils of World War II...

Yet, you never can really forget—ever. I know being separated from you is the most heart-breaking experience I could ever go through again...

Oh John, I know if anything ever happened to you I couldn't go on—Pat or no Pat. You're still first in my affections...

Yours is the greatest love. I bask in its warmth, even across the miles...

The two weeks after you shipped out and I didn't hear were sheer torture. And then—when I heard, it seemed as though you were close beside me again...

These years are strengthening our love and marriage. Nothing can tear us apart...

We have been fortunate in your assignments. You are non-active again, amphibious duty only. I am sure you'd tell me, for I'd rather know truth...

John, I can't stress enough that you are in Pat's thoughts. It amazes me...

This morning, Pat was having a party with her dolls. She suddenly left them, walked into the living room under your picture. Pat said, "I'm making supper for the kids (name for her dolls). You come home pretty soon. I'll make supper for you..."

It makes me happy that she includes you constantly in her speech...

I'd hate to count the number of times she's shown you her sore eye from yesterday's fall. Pat declared, "I went bumpety-bump downstairs Daddy—wasn't that funny?" And then—she laughed...

The ration board gave me an extra food stamp, so I expect to buy shoes and slippers for her in the city. I miss all the daily rituals like drawing your bath, mending your socks—oh, ever so much...

I think of you. Going to a show and a night club will be like heaven—the tomorrows for us...

Pat and I bask in the sunshine, dream of you, and when you'll be home. Imagine all the nice picnics, walks, or just hanging around in our backyard...

Now I must close, as Pat is getting up from her nap. I guess I'll just never be able to put into words any different way than just simply this: I love you. I love you...

It was March 17, 1945. Madre's vivid and forceful recollections were compelling. JJ was able to call, a quality time to capture and treasure. I reread the beginning of her letter that reached an imposing depth within my spiritual being...

So happy to get your call, yet so sad. I wanted to tell you to take care of yourself and keep well, that I'll always be awaiting your return...

I said none of these things! I know you heard me crying...

When you said goodbye, I heard the tears in your voice. If ever I wondered how I'd react to you going to war—I *know* now...

Later, I felt as though someone had carved my heart out with a knife. Damn this war—and its heartaches...

These last few days, I am feeling as I did when you first went into the service, completely lost and baffled...

Your mother told me to come this afternoon, eat with them. I couldn't even have a taste for food. Your mother was crying too...

Last night your voice broke on the phone. It was as though something snapped within me. Honestly, darling, it's hard on me, but unbearably hard for you...

I was as close to your folks today as I have ever been. Today, I looked at our Pat, and it seems her *every* motion is you…

She asked for you a lot and told me not to cry. She is one, swell kid…

Your sisters, Bridget and Helen, were so kind.…

Oh honey, please come back for a lot of "family." Oh, take care of yourself for Pat and I—we need you in our lives…

I hope you can cablegram me. The relief, knowing that you are safe, will be heart-lifting, if you know what I mean…

I'll keep the mail coming to you (F.P.O., v-mails, airmail weekly)…

It's as though there is no future ahead, but there *must* be…

I used Bridget's nail polish, Rosy Future. I said softly, "It looks hazy today, but I may as well make it bright." Bridget and Helen laughed…

God knows the loss of Joe. Now, Pete and you are both ok. Those realities are ample for any Mother and Dad to bear…

I feel very lucky that we met and had lots of memories to pile up before this war…

We'll survive as others have during such as separation and we'll one day—in '45 or '46 be reunited forever! Keep faith and hope until that day…

It was March 24, 1945. This letter was being read aloud by Helen, Dad's younger sister. The communication was from Pete, Dad's second sibling. Pete was also serving in different locales, seeing a lot of action in this war…

In another few days, it'll mark my 4th year in the service. Before you know it, I'll be in my 30's. What a *life*…

Enclosed you will find a check for $40 and a few snapshots taken in Nancy, France. The civilian is a Polish friend we met in that vicinity…

To date, I've received all your packages in excellent condition. Enjoyed it all tremendously. Again, I thank you for your thoughtfulness…

Give my love and best regards to Mother, Dad, Bridget, Marge, and Patty Jo—also brother John when you are writing to him…

Until we meet again—I remain your brother, Pete…

Madre wrote in a New York minute to my Dad—on the backside of Pete's letter. She wanted him to be able to read an exact copy of Pete's letter and whereabouts without delay…

Pete's letter sure made good time—airmail and not V-mail. It arrived in 8 days…Helen felt awful tonight. She found two Valentines in her pocketbook that were meant for you—one from her to her brother and the other from her folks for their son. Gee! It is too late to mail them now. I can see you laughing at me now, honey. I love you with all my heart and soul… Marge

It was still 1945. Madre wrote regularly to JJ. She kept the inspiring, rallying letters going outbound…

I realize you miss Pat and I like the devil. But, you sound like you have kept busier and contributing your part to the war effort…

You and the Newport chap must have had a wonderful reunion. It must seem like meeting someone from your home town…

I just know you'll be seeing an end to Japan before 1946 is out…

Things are brewing in the air, sweetheart. I can almost smell them around here and on the radio…

We'll be reunited before you know it—honestly! I feel like the Bible saying—my cup runneth over…

Can't you feel my love reaching out to you? Little Pat and I shall always be here waiting for the "three Karrs" to be complete again! I send all my love— Marge

Another one of Pete's letters to his sister hailed from Germany. Helen shared his reflections about the war and family love wishes with Madre. It was 1945 and the "unknowns of this war" still prevailed…

Dear Helen: Sorry for this day in writing home but just didn't have the time. Things around here are moving very swiftly…

Expect things to end in the another three months, then we'll have to start finishing another job. That means the C.B.I. (Madre guessed Conversion Battalion Infantry)…

You will find a check for $40.00. Just haven't found any use for money in this vicinity. The flowers and trees are in bloom. Sure is a pretty site, but for a few damaged homes…

This is only a short note to let you know—I'm still around…

Will close for the time being. Give my love to Mother, Dad, and the family… As ever, Pete Jr.

By April 29, 1945, there were rumors of a potential armistice. Madre decided spot on—pen another letter to her endearing JJ…

I suppose yesterday you were keyed up, as we were here with the false armistice report. Some people are of the opinion that something has *really* taken place…

Saturday night, places were crowded, as the announcement was declared *false* to prevent riots that could take place today…

Gee, darling, I felt so happy! And then—when it was *not* true, felt *so badly*…

Such a dull feeling—right where my heart is…

Oh, dearest—I hope by the time this letter reaches you, we shall have some good news…

Apparently, while conversing on the phone with Mary S, one of her neighbors, Madre found out that Germany had surrendered. She hung up quickly to verify the reports. Then she telephoned JJ's father…

His Dad cried with joy! My adorable Grandpa and Nana-to-be had just heard the news as well…

Three of their sons were fighting at the same time in World War II. JJ and Pete, Jr., who witnessed and survived harrowing experiences, returned home. All of the family harbored poignant memories and wrote to endearing sons or brothers—inspiring optimism and hope for ALL to return home safely…

Joe, the last-born sibling and a gentle soul, volunteered for the war efforts. He coveted his desire, becoming a fighter pilot. During the war, his plane was shot down. Joe's burial became the majestic ocean depths...

Later, the armistice reports were even contradicted. Nothing was really official. All of the family calmed down, but what a let down...

There was good news. Dad's folks got a letter from Pete Jr., written somewhere in Germany, dated April 17th. They were overjoyed, just to hear from him! Madre kept up her writing, this letter being written in pencil. It was November 2, 1945...

My dearest beloved: It is 11 p.m. and I am perched up in bed writing. If only I could talk to you right now. What brought all of this on? The movie called, "The Enchanted Cottage..."

See this movie, if you can or perhaps, you already have—Robert Young, Herbert Marshall, and Dorothy McGuire are the stars. The main theme is that if two people love strongly enough and deeply enough, they always will be beautiful to one another. Perhaps, not to the outside world, but to love one another—always...

Young—was a returning veteran flyer, badly disfigured. Dorothy—just a girl with a lovely voice, but homely face. These two found happiness in one another. Their faith and trust were encouraged by Marshall, a blind pianist from WWI...

There's much more to the whole picture, but I couldn't help but compare our supreme love life...

Oh John, I do so want you to know what a happy woman you have made me...

I am very glad you and I loved before this war...

Very glad we had a *solid* rock foundation *before* your entrance to World War II...

Patty Jo was far from a mistake. As you once said—she has cemented our marriage tighter and brought us closer together, if that is at all possible...

Signs of Cherubim blue and Seraphim red...
Comradery and angst with wartime efforts...
Beliefs of a better world beyond the horrors of war...

Anniversary Selections, Rites Of Passage, And Reflections: A Beloved Tradition

Back in 1948, this rallying, affective, and expressive man, my Daddy-to-be, elected to compose the beloved Anniversary letters. Now, at 67 years young, I owned ethereal images of my guardian angels.

"You and the autistic children—you see Madre and JJ's facial-cloud images with the jumbo sunglasses—like they wore in their elder years." My Reiki Grand Master was spot on...

Madre's words and gift of manila-clasped folders with special letters came full circle. There was the honoring—my "PJ three dots" for privacy or intimacy. And, of course, the PJ-you-will-know declarations of my perceptive Madre...

Here was a parental medley of joy, love, and contemplations—the excerpts from Anniversary letters. I felt an inner guidance and stillness. The telepathic transmissions from JJ and Madre kept unfolding and teaching me—as I reread and settled upon the distinctive excerpts in a touching synchrony. I was receiving counsel with the utmost reverence and homage...

Another testimonial dated January 1, 1949 was pulled out for reading. Amazing grace and finesse arrived in that moment. Madre *was equally as passionate as JJ in her quest to compose their beloved Anniversary letters...*

You and I are always close in our deep love and devotion, John. Somehow around Christmas and the New Year, the feelings become more potent…

Every year I think, "I couldn't be happier!" The next year rolls around and I find everything in our love and our daily life is richer, deeper, and finer! You do so much for me all the time, 365 days a year…

I shall always be your woman as I was in 1938…in 1959…in 1969…

Love you completely, now and always…

Madre and JJ initiated their marital bliss on New Year's eve, just before the "bong" of midnight jubilation. The precise date became the "wee hours" of New Year's Day...

As a child, adolescent, and young adult, I adored their story and ingenious timing. Mom's striking, ruby-red gown of soft velvet and Dad's posh, handsome suit were shown off. As a child, I played dress up in Madre's elegant wedding gown and lavish high-heels. They watched lovingly as I wobbled 'round and 'round to their special music...

There was only one minister during that wintry blizzard and their New Year's eve ceremony. My parents desired a cozy church near Hanover, New Hampshire—the beginning of their romantic saga. There were two intentions—that New Year's eve would never be forgotten and anniversaries would be extra special...

The mutual creativity and bonding of Madre and JJ blossomed from the onset. Possibly a nanosecond? The dreamscapes never eluded me in my PJ lifetime. But, in the now? I relished my novel, heartfelt images as their spiritual signs...

It was January 1, 1949. John, Johnny, JJ personified carpe diem—seizing the moment—to pen a special letter when their anniversary date drew near…

To my dearest wife on our anniversary— First, I love you, darling…

It has been swell living and loving you, and I am looking forward to the years ahead with youthful eagerness…

To marrying again—I would answer, "Sweetheart, without a moment's hesitation…"

An impassioned, intimate love letter followed. Near the end of this letter, my Dad heralded and praised the epitome of Madre's womanhood. He declared and honored how her passion of being and becoming contributed to a unique partnership…

There is my respect and honor of you as a woman of intelligence and companionship. You are everything a man would want in a woman…

You love and work with a man—a real partnership of marriage…

Every moment of life with you is an exciting adventure! I love it that way. You will hear no regrets on my part…

I look eagerly ahead to the rich years before us… Your devoted husband and love, Johnny

Anniversaries came and went, but the special letters were never forgotten. My parents' compositions solidified and dignified their intricate bonds. Their natural devotion and appreciation were obvious, an invaluable bestowal for us…

Friends and family members also acknowledged the uniqueness of their relationship in concert with an individuality. Once again, I recaptured Madre's declarations and encouragements…

I finally catapulted, recalling their love-sweet-love messages for our world in need of passionate caring and connections. I needed to pay forward their transformation, peaks, and valleys. Given my life

and evolution, the time was eminent—compost and communicate. Writing throughout 2018 and 2019, there was a shifting and transposing from the onset...

My words—what I have just penned—were still striking realizations. I had butterflies in my tummy. Excerpts of my parents' treasured thoughts and feelings were coming forth after decades. Pay forward, PJ...

To my precious, sweetest wife—Margaret. I want to thank you wholeheartedly for the swellest 10 years of my life… Eagerly awaiting the next 10…

Each year there appears to be some reason to cancel or postpone an appropriate gift to symbolize our union…

Suddenly, it came to me—we could not have a better gift to each other—our trusting and deep love. It is greater than any material gains…

I see in your eyes and daily actions… You are my *greatest asset*…

This day is a triple celebration—Patty, so healthy and happy—another on the way. And you—the best of all…

We are both very happy… Your eternally devoted Husband-Lover

Another just-pulled-out letter was dated January 1, 1956. I would have been four years old. What wondrous flashbacks, watching my mother in the living room. Madre sat at the chestnut desk, smiling intermittently as she wrote. Then paused and gazed, as if there were a million stars on our living room ceiling...

Madre scribed her pensive reflections in that 18th Anniversary letter—reminisces of their tough love and courageous attitude. There was Dad's ruptured disc, serious surgery, and a year-plus of recuperation...

Suddenly, my daily walks with Dad in his back brace triggered the vibrant images of my tiny fingers squeezing his seemingly gargantuan hand. And yes, my promises to Madre of "NO short cuts..." reappeared...

Wow, tiny PJ! At three and four years old, I became an equally determined spirit and caregiver. Madre was empathic beyond measure. There was another attribute that I recollected. Madre was a tough cookie when she decided, without any great fanfare, to speak her mind or write candidly...

I know the time is dragging for you and I am really sorry...

You are not a burden, John... This is something we are working out together...

Remember, it could be much worse. You could still be in a hospital away from your family...

Resolute Madre—often Margaret or Marge to my Dad— conveyed an uncanny "knowing" in these fearless letters. This time, she revived the urgency to slow up, release the stress...

She rejuvenated their united values of JJ changing jobs—for better physical health and healing. Ultimately, Madre affirmed that ALL concerns were the best and mutual adaptations for their cherished, growing family and relationship...

Solely, I want the best for you—to get well and have good health, but not just for a few months. I want you well always. The price is too high to go through this again...

I love you deeply. YOU ARE FIRST IN MY LIFE... Forever yours—Marge

It was January 1, 1958. I was a first grader, attending school in a small mill town located in western Massachusetts...

No preschools, no caregiving centers—just families trying "to make ends meet..." It was important to make quality time for picnics, local parks, and adventures in the Berkshires. Just enjoy—the precious, extended family relationships...

My attitude of gratitude resonated, especially with my "last-born PJ" flashbacks and mindfulness of Dad's Polish-Austrian, immigrant parents. They were the only Nana and Grandpa I would be able to adore and cultivate—a timeless love within the recesses of my heart...

I took one glance and smiled. My Dad's envelope was entitled— To a Grand Lady, My Wife! As always, it was a foreshadowing of his charming and indulgent moments of rejoicing...

My dearest one, it does not seem possible that 20 years has already slipped by...

It has been memorable and happy, despite some of the ordeals...

This day just doesn't connote a relationship to our wedding with the cold and a blizzard. Seems like we were married in the spring or fall...

Time means nothing, so long as we have each other and the results of our love...

As an aside—John, Johnny, JJ—presented Madre with a lavish corsage during the family celebration with us—the marveling kiddos. I was smitten with my nostalgic memories of these familial "anniversary" parties...

We melodramatic daughters would dress up in Madre's fancy dresses and fashionable high heels. Flaunting her ruby red lipstick until it was smeared upon our dinner napkins created the ultimate hysteria. Dad, with sweeping gestures and smiles, would pull out the dining chairs for each of his daughters—the drama princesses. Alas, my heart was a perceptive informant. I knew without a shadow of doubt. Madre deserved and received the biggest hugs and whopping smooches...

Seriously, my sisters and I took up the art of googling. Madre and JJ danced to big band music, ending with a splendid twirl, dip, and another lip-smacking kiss! Of course, the precious ohhhh-ahhhh's and our giggles came pronto...

Then one or two days passed. My parents would scoot out for the private celebration—Margaret and Johnny...

My oldest sister was the babysitter. Oh, the Broadway-style theatrics—the offbeat, visionary storytelling of three kids evolved. Ok, at least one precocious kiddo, PJ, was dramatizing a clever, utopian romance about my parents to the max! Over the years, my suave and debonair Dad—of an abundant heart and soul—would convey their dreamy courtship, whimsical enchantments, and fanciful stories of their private celebrations...

Someday, darling, I'll really give you a treat in our NH mountains—just the two of us, regardless of our sentimental dinners with family...

Think our day needs a special touch...

My Dad continued his poetic voice...my love, like a miser, nourishes the sustenance of life, to our living and basking in love...

There isn't a day that goes by when I don't thank my lucky stars in winning you for my wife and love. I'm deeply grateful as I see others about us....

Our love is much richer and stronger...

Darling, Happy Anniversary. Your lover and husband, Johnny

By now, I was picking out a stack of letters. I would select randomly, read, and chronicle the years in my final drafts. Today, I noticed January 1, 1959. I would have been seven years old...

Madre scribed an Anniversary letter about their twenty-one years of togetherness and appreciation of the adage "less is more." She was savoring the earlier Hanover and Ludlow days. I loved the way she recaptured their effortless dancing and swirling—in almost-perfect synchrony...

Dance Spirits of the Hanover night...

Spellbound connections and synchrony...

Vintage "Model T" adventures and fervent courtship...

We had so much fun with so little, darling… Our dancing as one…

I love you deeply tonight and every other 364 nights of our year to come…

May it be a better year for you. Please, lean on me a little, so I can help you at times…

Yours, Marge

I took a breather and mulled over my PJ-decades of experiencing diverse relationships—a soulmate in a long marriage, the divorce pendulum with transitions, and my dating chronicles. With the PJ revolutions and evolutions, certain chapters were closing…

It was a deliberate intention to ferret out the new beginnings—PJ, moving forward with brand-new courage. The process became a profound imprinting. One "aha" moment came naturally. All of our lives are colored with imperfect perfections…

I accepted that my parents had their share of stretching, strife, struggles with differences, and evolving. Without bias, Madre and JJ "worked out things" with a developing sense of dialogue and respect. I applauded their fortitude and individual moxie to attain a soul-filled marriage of almost 74 years…

It was January 1, 1961. On the envelope, there was an inscription, written in that exotic and bold scrawl of my Dad: To a lovely lady and devoted wife, your husband!

Dearest Marge: I am looking forward to our next year with almost the same youthful eagerness I had in 1938. I can't honestly explain the feeling of exhilaration…

Tonight, as I look across at you, I feel like a pioneer about to cut out a new career and home for the woman I love…

I would shout "yes" to let the whole world know how much I love and adore my woman. You are indeed a rare lady. There honestly aren't too many in this universe with your wonderful outlook on life….

Thank you a million times for all the words, work, and loving encouragement you have given me. I can never adequately express everything in words, but you understand in my embraces…

Never forget, sweetheart. You are the only one for me, couldn't possibly find a better mate…

I have been thanking my lucky star for twenty-four beautiful years, despite a few set-backs, and looking forward to many years with you. I want to take you dancing, to see a few plays, and take those moonlit walks…

I know you are looking eagerly for the same fulfillments. It's not an idle promise, darling. We will become a beautiful pair of loving newlyweds again…

I am anxious to house-hunt with you and plan for our own place…

I deeply feel this is our great opportunity to cut out a better piece of life for ourselves. I believe as you do that this is at least a step in the right direction…

The main thought—I love you very much and thank you…

It's a wonderful life with you. Bless you for saying, "Yes…"

It is my success! The rest will never match it, whatever I achieve in life…

I adore and love you, my wife… Your loving husband, Johnny

Four years later, the eureka or epiphany could not be missed. Once again, Dad's inspirational reflections were penned. Marveling moments were heightened, regardless of a lifetime rapport with my Dad…

The reading experiences could have felt surreal. Instead, I was drawn consistently—to the calming, soothing, and meditative breaths. I savored and honored the adulation, allegiance, and evolving saga of Madre and JJ…

It is January 1, 1965. It is another Anniversary letter, full of empowering leaps of faith and abundance…

That wonderful day has arrived again and refreshed glorious memories of yesteryears…

The horizons have brightened considerably for us…

We can truly begin living a wonderful and full life. I am truly enjoying our home and the wonderful friends we are making through your efforts…

I truly marvel at your rapid assimilation of church, friends, and the entire elite' class of our new environment. You are wonderful…

Frankly, we have joked about potentials, but you astound me. I just wonder whether "yours truly" can keep up with you. You are really running a hard race and I am amazed at your spirit. It's glorious, darling….

My new position has many challenges. I really eat them up and look for more—mainly because the incentive is there to obtain more for us to enjoy life together, Margaret…

I am yours devotedly, Margaret

It was 1966. An Anniversary letter was enclosed in an envelope that denoted: Just for You and To the Most Lovable Wife and Sweetheart…

Today, just a few hours before the bells toll the Anniversary hour of our happy marriage, I had the urge to write you again. Somehow, I want to reach the innermost heart and mind…

For just this moment, I want to possess the talents of Shakespeare or Bernard Shaw to reveal the depth of my need and love for you, especially this year of our lives… Since my literary talents can't express the core of my feelings, please let me telegraph them…

My love is even stronger. All our experiences and living have only tended to strengthen our love…

Happy anniversary and many, many more to come. I want to celebrate them all with you…

Your lover and adoring husband

Fast forward—another two years—to greet the richness and grandeur of 1968. JJ, Johnny, John—was relishing, luxuriating, and embellishing the amazing grace of thirty years! Their mutual striving and energy, gratitude, and dreams had come to a noteworthy fruition, another gratifying and mature actualization…

It just doesn't feel like 30 years have slipped away…

Time has only cemented a stronger bond of love. I never dreamed in my youthful devotion that a man could adore and love a woman—a real part of his physical, spiritual, and emotional self...

Dreams, energies, expectations, and ambitions. Every facet of my thoughts revolve about our beautiful union...

You have given me much courage and support in all my endeavors...

This is one man who will readily admit that his loving wife had a great deal to do with his growth in many areas...

My Dad's letter became a continuum of their transitions and testimonials. He lauded their sense of oneness, an ultimate union. I was swayed and stirred in the same moment, as JJ's writings embodied the self-expressions of today—the realm of spirituality and like-mindedness...

The late 1960's represented an earlier period in society when these expressions were a rarity. I sensed and accepted my next spiritual, telepathic message. Both of my parents divulged that they were ahead of their time. They brought into being—a courage and spirit to expand their universe with an acceptance of that truth...

My only prayer at this very moment—you, too—have felt the same *and* total commitment to my being...

Thank you many times for saying "yes" and loving me for all these years...

I am looking forward to another 30-plus years... Your devoted husband

The 1971 Anniversary letter was intimate and private. A later context in this letter included an invitation, chock full of the capitalizations. Dear JJ loved to scrawl in this infamous, letter-writing style. I recalled immediately—JJ often used that same flair in our yearly birthday letters—much to our chagrin and delight...

To 'THE' Girl in MY LIFE, Margaret...

I request the honor and privilege of your charming company for a REAL Private Dinner—just the two of us, after family activities have tempered down….

I eagerly await your affirmative answer. PLEASE don't delay…

I LOVE YOU DEARLY! However it happened, our chance meeting, your first reluctance…

I am indebted completely to that unknown force of nature or God which brought us together…

This beautiful union to me, it is a full expression of my love for you…

THIRTY-TWO wonderful years have passed and I hopefully pray as many, as if not more, will be granted us…

In closing—Margaret—all I want to say is, "Will you marry me as readily and eagerly as you did the FIRST time? My answer would be a very loud— "YES!" for the entire world to hear…

Their thirty-third Anniversary in 1973 accentuated a symbolic keepsake. There was a value of an enduring union in a world of different statistics, namely divorce and separation. Their vows were to hang tough and go for broke—on their marital journey of hills and valleys…

Persistence, leave no stone unturned, authentic caring, and an untapped reserve of energy to stay-the-course were transparent throughout my lifetime. It came as no surprise—what I was rereading in this letter…

It is an awesome thought at times when you compare us with the limited statistical successes that articles relate about marriages, happiness, and love enduring through time. Yet, here we are just as excited about each other as the first days of our romance…

Many times, as I look back over the hills and valleys we have travelled together, I have been amazed by the wonderful accomplishments of our life—our home, the children, and our love for each other…

I realize that much of the successes have been due to that *undefinable quality of spirit and love* that you, Margaret, carry throughout our life…

Without you, things would not be the same. You have sparked this union's flame to grow eternally… I am humbly proud *and* grateful to be your husband…

Man is such a mischievous boy in many ways. He never really grows up despite his worldly appearances and successes…

It takes a loving, knowing, and compassionate woman of great understanding, like you, to make him truly a man each step of the way…

My only hope is that I have given you as much happiness, joy, and love to balance the scale as you have given me…

In 1975, their life frontier was changing. By this 35th Anniversary, the discovery of Madre's benign pituitary tumor realigned their wayfaring and adventures. First, it was the onset of partial eyesight and CAT scans without answers. Second, it was JJ's undying research at libraries and additional medical consults. Finally, another CAT scan revealed Madre's large tumor that warranted urgent surgery…

There were two famous doctors in Boston with a new, reputable technique. An acclaimed woman doctor on hormonal balancing for the rest of Madre's life was also a team player in her recovery. Without any hesitation, the simpatico love of our family ensued. JJ was the vanguard in Madre's healing process…

This Anniversary is especially *precious*, for your personal problems *really* rocked me. It was an experience I never anticipated…

The reality of losing YOU before we even had the glorious, exhilarating joys of old age, and the mutual happy play times with our potential grandchildren, truly shook me to the core…

Now, you cannot possibly envision my happiness seeing you make a marked progress for the better…

I know that we must watch your continual efforts to retain those positive results…

Events have made me more aware of our deep love and devotion to each other…

You can rest assured that every effort I expend will be for that end—more determination and positive action than ever before…

Journey of innate healing...

A fearless release of finesse and creativity...

Revitalization and renewals with impassioned art...

My mother was an innate healer in her own right. Her journey with impassioned art—oil paintings—revealed a flair, finesse, creativity, and provided the timely revitalization and renewal. Painting expanded her "stillness within" way ahead of any New Age or Zen catalysts. Oil painting became a serene reawakening and fearless release from the onset of her unexpected tumor, the major adjustments, and the ongoing radiation...

The two famous and humble surgeons provided hope—for a full recovery. My parents' love and daily encouragements magnified a glowing beacon for my lifespan inheritance—a spiritual awareness of the emanating light of life-force energy, healing, and verve to move forward together, no matter what happened...

You don't know how it pleases me to see you get so much personal sense of satisfaction and achievement with your paintings, Margaret. So much of YOU is poured forth and revealed....

A very important phase of our efforts is drawing us into a new, totally exhilarating adventure—the impending union of our last seedling *(yep, that was me)...*

I am so happy that we have been most fortunate to help and be active in these events....

My personal concern has shown with our third blessing *(yep, that was me)...*

We have done our best to give our adult children, our three daughters, the base and abilities to cope with their problems...

Today, on OUR DAY, I hope the weather favors us, so that we may leisurely tour to a pleasant spot, sit down together for dinner, and muse together for the FUTURE...

It can't be anything but WONDERFUL...

Wherever fate draws us, I know that it will be a very happy life, for I will have YOU by my side. That alone is the most important fact in my life....

TODAY, I pledge undying love—first quoted in our wedded vows. Their meaning has grown within me as we moved thru life together....

Earlier, I lived in a cloud of Joy that you wanted me for your mate, without truly savoring the depth of their text *and* deep meaning….

Recovery was tenuous, a new pathfinding for the famous doctors and all of us. Four years of mountain tops and ravines finally passed. In the interim, my Dad was devoted—scripting the constant, loving-kind letters to Madre…

The glorious, unfathomable "now" was a harbinger of 1979. My parents' Anniversary bliss was captured with expressions of new-found resilience, purposeful dreamscapes, and noble vows of the rousing enrichments to be…

As I view and weigh the retiring years of decisions and activities of both friends and acquaintances, the more determined is my mindset NOT to spend useless days with no increasing strengths of purpose or love in our relationship…

To sit and allow time to march parallel with the remaining beats of the heart is just a fast race to boredom between two people and life itself….

With the strengths of our love and growing dreams, let us take this point of life, and this Day, Our Day, to renew our Vows of Love and Aspirations…

Let us build openly and together—an even richer life of accomplishments, both individually and as loving partners…

Let us say to each other—openly, the unspoken thoughts of truths rather than allow them to smolder within so that we may, in all sincerity, move together in directions destined to inspire the basis of new adventures and enriched satisfactions…

Let it be said in the winds of time—they loved, worked, dreamt, and achieved with some small measure of accomplishment…

Perhaps, not enough to effect a mark in the evolution of human life, but they tried…

Whatever mysterious forces drew us together and helped to solidify our love, they did not err…

But, I must acknowledge and credit us for working together with understanding to build upon those good fortunes…

Deep within me, I know we will continue to add to our love—unspoken, but understood…

I am looking forward to a LONG FUTURE together, even richer in blends of our love, if that is possible…

I, for one, accept the CHALLENGE to make it a REALITY! To our love and future, John

On JJ's birthday in 1981, Madre wrote in a calligraphic style. On her envelope was, "What a memory to treasure! I loved Opryland. Thank you for the Big Detour, so I could enjoy the adventure." Inside this envelope, Madre shared a tribute of anticipation, their wealth of giving, and her attitude of gratitude. I paused purposefully for a reason…

I had written a 2012 book entitled, "Tango On." My subtitle came pretty much without conscious thinking or effort. Attitude = Altitude. Shortly after its publication, my kindred spirit Madre remarked that she really valued the nitty-gritty of my book. To her, gratitude was an action. Madre took pride and ownership of her soaring, this sky-high state of being. Gratitude and the "tango on" spirit were obvious as I continued to read about their anticipated retirement…

Your birthday letter was such a warm one with anticipation of our retirement years. I, too, have the "gut feeling" that God will grant us this as a very enjoyable time of our lives…

As we are traveling on the road, I cannot make you an actual cake, but I have made many cakes for you over the years…

You are, as you say, a quiet man at times—but such a good one with your untiring love and support. I know we will make mutual decisions about our retirement years ahead…

We will make plans to see new sights. So happy—we are so mutual about travel and liking to do many of the same things constantly…

Thank you for asking me to marry you and giving me so much happiness along the way!

Some things never change with time—children go barefoot, jonquils grow in spring, babies still reach upward to adults, meadowlarks still sing and heavenly stars shine above…

The world has more need of gentle hearts and love that are warm and true like yours…

Your thoughtful deeds make the world a better place with your kindness and ever-giving love to me, our children, and now—our grandchildren…

All will bring you joy the whole year through, not just one day…

I don't want to inflate your ego too much, but does take special qualities to make a husband like you—a gentle manner of a true and trusted person with a vast amount of patience that never seems to know no end…

I love you deeply and admire these traits all year…

You give your children good advice, but you also know that your children need to think things out for themselves, form their own conclusions…

There are times when our children must do the talking (and you let them!)…

Our children have loved you for a "friend" instead of just a Dad…

Emerson said, "Though we travel the world over to find the beautiful, we carry it with us or we find it not." How true and this applies to you, John with all of your giving…

You recall our favorite plaque about walking our journey—called life with a purpose—calling it our own. It's beneath picture of two children hand in hand, walking down a winding road…

Our PJ found this "gem" right after she attended University of New Hampshire…

So happy to be with you on your 66th. Yours forever!

It was the next year and the "new beginnings" arrived with their Anniversary of 1982. Madre was well into recovery, now able to pen the traditional and "special" letter—to her Dearest John…

Forty-four years is a long time. God has granted us time, health, and a future… Needless to say, I want to make 45+ years of happiness with you…

My physical upset gave me plenty of 'thinking and reflecting time' lying in a hospital bed day after day and unable to read…

It made me doubly realize the love and devotion of our whole family unit, plus your patience and understanding and deep love…

All of our family devotion sustained me with a strong will to recover. I am only human and had a few bad moments. Those moments have been erased with time and strength. I love you on our 44ᵗʰ because I'm *still here*…

It is a warm, peaceful feeling…to have you as my husband and lover! My three wishes for you on this Our Day—and, may they come true: 1) a loving wish for happiness 2) that life will always be as wonderful and good to you as you have been to me and 3) a special one—that we shall *never* part and that you'll always share with me the love that is in your heart…

Once again, Emerson's prose comes to mind. "Though we travel the world over to find the beautiful, we must carry it with us or we find it not." Because of YOU, I always have the beautiful with me….

My memories and love are centered in a Husband that I just think the world of… You make things right, you give constantly, you share, you listen, and you care! It makes my heart sing…

May we never lose sight of our dreams, John—that we both shall remain alive to life as we are today, even as we age gracefully…

Our togetherness and growth will always be there because we are able to have such a "special day" without a lot of material gifts every year…

I look forward to our special candle-lit dinner and our quiet New Year's Eve—and then our special New Year's Day….

We have such a wealth of love, devotion, and just being US…

I love you until eternity… Yours forever—Marge

I pulled out another manila folder that was shouting (sic) from the back of my bedroom closet each time I opened the door. The 1989 letter echoed the poignant, unfeigned messages. It was composed by Madre on a revered Anniversary...

As each day becomes light, you can depend upon the sun to rise. With each sunrise, as I gaze at you, I know we have another brand new day ahead...

I know that love is our most precious gift. May it always shine upon us...

One day you may be the one to scatter my ashes to the winds and to let the flowers grow. Remember me with a kind deed or word to someone who loves you deeply, namely our three daughters, and then I will live forever in your heart and soul...

Your red ruby ring, the treasured gift from your Dad, is a symbol and ring of precious gems. As your birthstone, it fits you as a special person, for it represents passion, vitality, and exuberance, adding lots of "color" to our lives...

Every morning you make my day, trying to get me wide awake and I enjoy every minute of it...

I still pinch myself—51 years later, we have each other...

I can be a difficult person to get along with, but that comes by having to be independent at an early age and making decisions, not having a "Dad" and Mother is sometimes hard to relate to...

Hang around with me—my John—I am still a small "country girl" at heart...

Happy in our inner, cozy little home—our castle! I would change nothing of my deep, abiding love...

My unconditional love reaches way down into the soul...

I feel so deeply for you, until my last breath and beyond...

Their 55th Anniversary had commenced. Madre and JJ fashioned the "special" letters to each other, acknowledging the metamorphosis—of an unconditional love...

I witnessed that my parents searched for a balance of the pinnacles and swale throughout their decades of a loving-kind journey. More than ever in my lifespan, certain attributes resonated in my persona.

As individuals, my parents valued intuition. Together, Madre and JJ pursued the mystique of charismatic virtues, charm, and surprising chemistry encountered along any of the winding or unforeseen roads...

JJ wrote to his Bride: I honestly can't fathom the passing of 55 wonderful years together. We are darned *Lucky* in spite of the negatives along the way, but then it makes us appreciate all the cherished, good experiences of our life...

We are extremely lucky in family, far beyond normal expectations, if compared to people we know who are ignored at this stage of life...

You have given so much of yourself to us, unselfishly and beyond the norm...

As I daydream and look back at events, "you" and *you alone* have been the driving force in our successes...

You have inspired and encouraged us. You still do. Our faces lighten up at the sight of you...

It is as it should be, for it was your fierce determination to form a solid base as your love, mind, and drive could fashion. Today, all of us enjoy the rich benefits...

Your support and encouragement pushed me to achieve and add to your efforts. Together, we formed a solid foundation...

I am certain our children will work out their individual problems, thanks to the basics established by you in their formative years. We tried to set examples and it has established guides for them to fashion their lives...

I love you so much—it really is a *wonderful* hurt in my Heart. Thank you, darling...

Truly look forward to more years on this earth with you. Your lover boy, John

P.S. Don't forget the 55th Dartmouth reunion in Hanover and that favorite song of ours—All of me...Why don't you take all of me...

Without whistles, fanfare, or nudges, I experienced the sentimental flashbacks. Michael Buble's rendition of this song—All of Me—was played at their wakes, memorial services, and on the compelling DVDs that my sister and I created...

There was a vision of my childhood—watching my Mom sing that tune to my Dad. And, of course, JJ was smiling and contributed confidently to the melody. Then I beheld my fast-forward images of Madre singing in her 90's...

The technicolor images, like a precious film, portrayed a favorite volunteer at her nursing home. Maurice performed regularly with his accordion—to entertain, engage, and spread the joy...

"All of Me" was part of his musical repertoire, especially for my endearing mother. My sister and I nodded. We recaptured—in a nanosecond—my parents and their animated, wistful sing-a-longs of their beloved "All of Me"...

I paused for three, meditative breaths. Then I went back to reading about their awe-inspiring time—55 staggering years. On this writing day, I immersed myself into these decades with Madre's earmarked letter to her dearest John...

Fifty-five wonderful years! Dearest John—I have to pinch myself to realize we have attained this goal. How blessed we are to *still* have one another…

We have met each other's needs in times of stress as well as happiness. That has cemented such a strong, everlasting bond…

I glow and bask in your deep love. I am truly somebody. You make me feel that daily…

We have a lovely, devoted family and they are a part of our love and creation…

After all these years—to choose the same cards only proves how deep and close our thoughts are for one another, so blended. There is no art of living together, we are a natural team…

Never worry about those lottery winnings. I feel RICH just having you as a husband, lover, and friend…

No two people can possibly live together in an intimate, emotional relationship without sometimes frustrating each other, but our understanding is there…

We have a healthy growth for each other. Differences in our energy and physical abilities have come about with aging, but we accept and work them out...

You are such a good father—gentle but firm. You respect our daughters' independence and our teachings...

Our girls have needed models rather than critics, as they age gracefully with us. Their love and life choices will survive...

I chose prose excerpts to end my letter, John. Our lives came together blending in an assured tranquility—a freshness, newness, and enchanting excitement of discovering each other...

Love was there the day we met—strong and enduring, and now, I love you more than I ever have... We shall always be as *one*. My love—forever, Marge

It was January 1, 1995. JJ could not imagine anything better than to scribe a "spellbound" Anniversary letter. I was drawn to a first-class synchrony—unique partnership, mutual respect, nurture our love, and worth every struggle....

Looking back, a tapestry of family sacrifices...
Ludlow days tempered, illuminating new beginnings...
Familial blueprints change and evolve for the future...

I hovered in a remarkable abyss. My PJ cup runneth over with JJ's beguiling beliefs—promises of daily love and his grandiose finale—devotion into eternity…

My eyes have welled with grateful tears and readings. I basked in this synchronistic rhythm created with their lifetime values—take leaps of faith, conquer human fears, grab onto optimism to fuel conviction, and pursue the yen of becoming. I reread JJ's composition about partnership and serenity…

I marvel at the serenity in this unique partnership, and the respect we have for each other. We have worked hard at this union and thus, find it full of richness and satisfaction…

Even at this stage of the game, we don't hesitate to put forth the effort, knowing well that the aging process creates other challenges to meet…

We sustain and nurture the love of our youth and maturing process…

I can truly say today, it was worth every struggle to win your attention and love and to dissolve the notion that I was a "Pin-Head" as your grandmother classified Dartmouth students…

Now, there is much more to see and enjoy together—trips and places to go—adventures to relish and record for our old age, a period when the rocking chair will appear to be more desirable than longer journeys and adventures…

I hopefully envision us beyond the century mark…

I shall join you in a "toast" for a love stronger than it was in the beginning, if that is possible.

I love, admire, and cherish you, Margaret—always will to eternity…

Your husband and lover, John

It was January 1, 1996. I was already daydreaming of my perusal of heartrending Anniversary letters. Yet, I was taken off guard…

My Dad wrote of my illness, their parental angst and prayers for my healing and survival. Later in my lifespan, as a Reiki-Shamballa master with beholden clients, I sensed their beliefs enfolding me from a mystical, ethereal level...

I reread my Dad's letter differently with my Reiki-Shamballa and Jitsu influences. Enlightenments for the mind, body, and spirit came forth. Grace emanated from my heart chakra. There was a new solace with my "stillness" within and daily meditations...

I am richer in many ways too numerous to detail, BUT I can do it if you insist...

This year has been pierced with a bit of sadness with our youngest daughter's unfortunate illness. All of us have felt the deep pangs of sadness and dismay for PJ...

It is not an easy matter to set aside and we can't do much to right the situation. BUT, I say with deep, firm fate, *PJ will find the path to recovery...*

We are all fighters, once we set our mind to the right path. All our combined messages, prayers, and efforts to support PJ will strengthen her own strengths and desires to conquer this setback. I know *and* feel it...

Tonight, two loving parents and lovers over the many years, will send vibrations and blessings—in the mystical air waves. She will feel them, for you and I created this child...

My love—on our 59th union together... I love you passionately and forever...

The arrival of another January 1st in 1998 was equally resplendent with matters of the heart. Madre created her benevolent letter to JJ, recounting their spirit-filled blessings...

Again, I was taken off guard. Madre expressed jubilance with her "surprise" diamond ring on the 50th Anniversary. A mysterious journey to New Hampshire, a let's-go-inside enticement, and the indulgence of a decades-in-the-waiting diamond..."

JJ was unable to afford the diamond he yearned to give Madre during the early courting days. He was washing hospital floors for college funds and to aid his parents' financial burdens. It was Madre's next story of two lovebirds and her wishes...

Fast forward to her nursing home. Madre was vibrant in her early 90's, expressing her final wishes—about what jewelry she wanted my sister and I to wear—whenever she passed on and joined her soul-mate, JJ...

She owned a few bejewels. They were in a delicate, blue box encased with a decadent, gold trim. My sister was to receive her "birth-stone" ring set in fine gold, representative of each daughter's birthday. I was to receive Madre's 50th rapture—the "surprise" diamond ring from JJ—on that mysterious journey to New Hampshire...

When I did receive this "rock," our favorite acclaim for JJ's surprise, I attempted to put the diamond on a few fingers. I tried my index, middle, fourth, and then finally—my baby finger...

This moment in life took my breath away. The diamond fit perfectly on my fourth finger, just like Madre's wedding ring. Oh my... I began to cry softly, missing their sweet essence and knowing I could not wear Madre's "rock" on that finger...

Later, my sister queried if I was wearing and enjoying Madre's diamond ring. I confessed—why I let the "rock" rest in peace in Madre's beautiful, blue box. My sister declared the need for Plan B immediately. Carpe Diem! I seized that moment and Plan B, went to our entrusted jewelers, and sized the "rock" for my PJ pinky-finger...

Now? I wear my pinky-finger, diamond "rock"—on special occasions and "just because..." The glistening diamond hovers there, symbolically close to Madre's wedding-band finger. In soft repose and my heartfelt quietness, I resumed the reading of Madre's letter...

We are blessed to have one another at this stage of many happy years, John. I am thankful every day—we see the sunrise together. It is peaceful, comforting…

You are my closest friend and confidant along with being a wonderful, attentive, and very supportive husband…

You wake me up every day. All we need is our great love to sustain us through struggles *and* happy moments—of which we have had many—*more* than we can count…

Every day I admire the 50th diamond you gave me. It is a part of my body, goes with me everywhere—your LOVE…

Our love is being passed around (as PJ thanked us). We are such a united family…

As you told me last year, our love and adventures make each anniversary the "New Beginning" to go onward…

This year, more than ever, we need one another to face 1997 with our youngest PJ—and pray for an improvement with her incapacitating health. We had her with us last year at this same time. Very special…

Truly, we have a lot to be grateful for, especially that we can write lovingly to each other at this stage…

I shall make you our annual dinner. I love doing that … My one and only!

The next year was reserved for a "WOW" reading. JJ's bold capitalizations were for his exaltations and euphoria…

January 1, 1998. WOW! Marge, the more I dwell upon it, the more WOW'S pour out of my lips. I attribute our success to YOU! I marvel at your achievements with our family…

Now—just THINK—about OUR FAMILY. Where else is there a family with so much individual independence? Even Patches, our family dog, would agree. Each stands their Ground, yet truly loves one another, and would step in to support one another—a fight to death, if the need arose…

We, as parents, get irked when we try to advise and get "flak." But, we *unite* some way to a Common Ground. I guess the latter is one of our bases of success…

We *love too much* to hold any grievance—a step taken to hold a richer treasure—our Love…

The tango of life, together like the dance, how else could you describe our relationship? It is a story of passion from the day of our first dance together…

Life has been kind to us in spite of the rough spots along the way…

I thank you in advance for the years ahead—together…

Your Man, John, for Life! P.S. Note the stamp—a supersonic flight to your Heart

Most people would not look for the envelope designs. Yet, the manila-clasped folders with letters in envelopes often displayed creativity, a romantic flair, humor, and "catch" phrases. Madre's Anniversary letter of 1995 was no exception…

Her envelope was entitled, "To John—My One and Only!" Her sketch, just the profile of a man, was compelling artistry to behold…

Dearest John—We are so blessed to have our health and deep love for one another at this stage of our lives. We have lost individuals very close to us this past year, which makes me treasure our union and survival even more…

Odd that our youngest daughter (that was me, living in the Southwest) wrote about "reflections," because my card depicts just that—like a "spirit" borne within us moving across many miles…

I call it a *miracle*—just as I have felt meeting you years ago and turning my whole life into a different pattern, a wonderful one over the years…

We have our special dinner and letters which I read and reread all year long—one days lasts *forever* to the next year. As you stated last year, "we blend well together and our love grows stronger with time…"

You called me the "star" in your life. We've reached for all of them—some we've captured in our happiness and, yes, in our struggles. There are more *stars* out yonder for us to discover…

Our character develops as our youth fades and our mode of conduct, fortitude, and integrity makes us something special in our children's eyes—and, even in our grandchildren's lives…

January is the month where we can tune out the world—hibernate a little, read books, have a rich beef stew or homemade soup to comfort our souls…

The winding road is there for us. All that matters is that we still have one another…

All the lessons we learn as we travel these paths together! Our "All of Me" song is our connection of enduring love…

We blend deeply. We tolerate one another very well in our senior years—eh? Yours forever

STRONG
& FIERCE

"All of Me" rendition evolves...
Enduring love, traversing their peaks and valleys...
Strong and fierce, this Margaret and Johnny...

Madre set about to compose and amplify feelings, never tiring of the tradition of "special" letters. In 1996, time was marching forth with the contentments. Madre's 58th Anniversary card highlighted the lofty, sustained bonding...

This card—just the right thoughts! We do indeed blend together over a long period of years and time. Our love does seem to grow stronger every year...

Like yesterday—you buy me a love bouquet. Your eyes, as you present the bouquet, are so *full* of love and adoration...

God has blessed us with this long unity which shows in my peaceful and contented face. We are there for each other, every step of the way...

You do cater and spoil me, but I love every minute of it. Our strong unity will be there through struggles of illness. We'll meet each other's needs...

You have such a positive attitude and most of all, a sense of humor...

Every struggle has drawn us closer, even our three grandchildren. I know we've known a success that some families never achieve...

You always seem to thank me for creating a close family, but my darling, you were always there when I needed you with our children's problems—your love and *strong* support...

Our small celebrations have grown over 58 years—almost a *miracle*...

Our girls recall dressing up in gowns to compete for their Dad's affections. This year we have one of them, our youngest PJ, with us to make it even warmer...

I recall the war years and your *safe* arrival home. I recall trying to do an anniversary dinner on a "shoe string" but was so happy...

We had love and passion, our richest assets. And, only a victrola rested on the floor to dance by with a few records...

"Star Dust" and "All of Me" were treasured when our love was cemented long ago. That strong *spark* still exists...

Marriage has many expressions—each one of LOVE—quiet evenings, music playing, you and I in our favorite chairs reading, pages turning. Therein lies my true happiness and contentment—knowing you, my love, are there for me…

I love sharing my life with you now and forever. You are the ONLY MAN in my life—how wealthy it makes me *feel inside*…

Always your wife, lover, and friend. Yours 'til eternity, Margaret

JJ's Anniversary letter to Madre included a charming, irresistible card. These 1996 tributes represented their courageous co-existence across the decades…

Even if I were not their daughter, there was need of brief hiatus to ascertain the entirety of vibration—adulation, sanctity, and venturing to places—known and unknown. Such frankness and free spirit, holistic thoughts about one's mind and soul, were indeed a rarity for their generation…

There is still much to sample and see in Life. The open road to new memories…

To MY Woman, who made and still is making a Big Adventure of life together. I see this Spirit in our girls, even in their offsprings…

It's adventure in a meaningful way, both thru accomplishments in life as well as adding a little mischievous fun—spice is what you called it…

Like a top chef, you have been that ingredient added to the "Mix" which gave life together a new meaning…

We have worked and loved together, grasping each rung of our ladder of Dreams. In the tough times, you loved and inspired us to try and surmount the obstacles…

Today, we have learned to nudge each other gently and lovingly, to take heart and to do our mind's boldness of spirit and adventure…

I suspected all of this from the very beginning when we pledged ourselves to each other and confronted the road to Concord, NH—a road covered by a blizzard of snow and swirled by a cold wind—making it a dangerous adventure for two "madly in love…"

Two nuts, determined to reach our honeymoon lodging…

We can't sit still, you know. It's our restless love, adventurous urges, and Spirit that make each anniversary the *New Beginning* together, adding to "Our Book" of a long life together…

Are you ready to kick up your heels? You know they are playing "Our Song!" I love "you" darling for the woman you were and are thru our life…

We did it "Our Way" together! Floor the gas pedal and Let's Go… With All My Love, John

It was 1998. Madre's letter heralded the deep-seated awareness of a divine sanction—60 years of their "unique togetherness." There was a quiescent resonance and that returning mystique, an astonishment of how they reached such a place and time…

Their soulmate journey, regardless of the provocations, was a glorious celebration. The paths revealed an uncommon, salient focus on commitment. Plus their steadfast rises, abiding inspirations, and allegiant determination during strife or pain were a testament to the imperfect perfections in humankind…

Can you believe we made it to our 60th Anniversary? Today, I realized hanging onto letters—all important—that I should make up a "special box" to hold ALL. They go back to age 10 and younger with our loving daughters…

Such a history of LOVE—we are blessed! Our "Big 60th" in Hanover at Dartmouth College is forthcoming. I feel that we shall be one of fortunate couples to make it…

Recall "The Pops" and Gershwin's music favorites that we used to dance to…

No one can snatch away any memories…

I bless the day I met and fell so deeply in love, that even as I pen this letter, I feel a deeper and passionate feeling of oneness…

I felt that with the birth of each child—such a closeness—and, they are all LOVE children. It is apparent in their diversified personalities…

Our youngest—PJ—made us feel the distance this year and we'll reread her thoughts over and over again! The huge separation of mileage to Texas is hard to manage at times—on the part of us *and* her…

Browning once said, "Take away LOVE, and our earth would be a tomb." How very true! Please know I'll love you to eternity…

In the after life, your spirit and closeness will always be with us forever…

I shall prepare our wonderful "tradition" of a New Year's dinner at home…

I am the wealthiest woman in the world…

Another year passed, but never without a letter. This reality manifested an intuitive catalyst within the alcoves of my heart. As I read and dwelled upon the power of JJ's written words, I was beholden for his universal appeals…

Immersion in talented writing groups and my books had sparked the rekindling of a fuller awareness about the gift of written words. JJ's letter reinforced the real world phenomenon. Pen-to-paper trails would always beget a clarity, efficacy, and exactness—way beyond our "gist of memories" that lingered, weakened, or withered across time and space…

Little did I know, JJ's poignant words and conjured images would whet a new appetite for something else. Suddenly, I wanted to seize omnipotent images of Madre and myself—our dialogic communiques, truths, and holding hands…

It was the day that I tucked Madre's gift of manila-clasped folders close to my chest. We tossed our butterfly kisses as I departed for home. What a consummate day of words and images. I was deeply moved by an earnest messenger—my benevolent Madre…

I paused momentarily while writing this chapter. The communiques and imagery almost seemed surreal. Then I accepted the stillness that embodied my being in the exact moment. When I eventually resumed my immersion with JJ's letter, an advanced consciousness became my next gift...

My extraordinary wife: Each minute and hour with you is a treasure of wonderful memories, adding to a mountain of them through the years...

You know what, my darling wife and partner, I am eager for more years of togetherness and unexpected adventures...

Put that Scottish defiance to work, cruising your body's cells with a cry—Come on, come on—keep this beauty going, fuel all the engines. YOU are special...

I don't want to RUSH the TIME, but I can't seem to slow it up...

You are like a *rare wine*, you drink slowly—rolling over all the taste buds of life...

You have so much to offer for happiness and life. You have brought three lovely daughters into our life. They have developed into rare creatures like yourself...

Time and realities of life together have made me strongly aware of what a treasure you are. Yes, my love for you still grows each minute...

Hopefully, love is beyond the body life, into the spiritual world of the unknown. Your mate to Eternity...

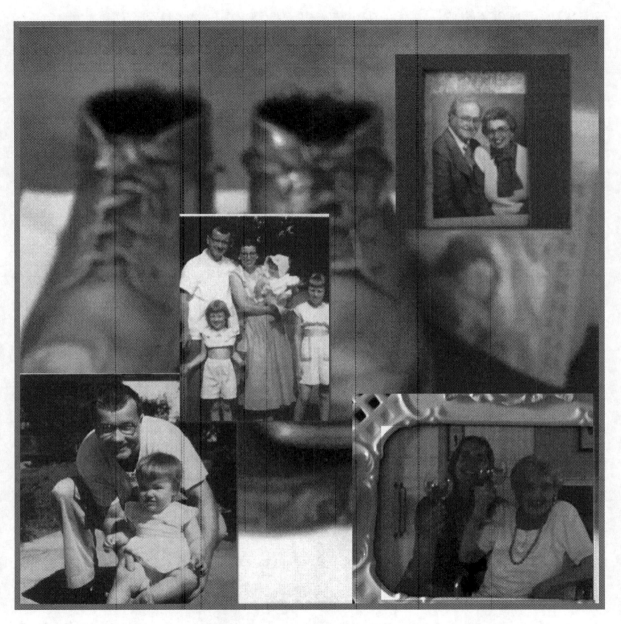

All the taste buds of life...
Three daughters, resilient and independent...
Unconditional love and respect become the hues of
marital bliss and an indomitable Spirit...

Fast forward in time—to 2000... Madre struggled to write legibly to beloved JJ, her daughters, and dear friends, given the escalating pain of osteoarthritis. Ready or not, the 62nd anniversary became a prophecy for the challenging "rites of passage." Family health conditions were holding steady at the port, but other trials would be drifting inward with the intermittent sea mists...

Madre's health issues started to decline, but not her attendant spirit. My Dad's successful prostrate surgery at 83 years young was presented in a medical journal. Alas, my chronic vestibular-neurological relapses and urgency for avant garde medical teams had lessened...

The "Life is Good" slogan was like a neon light for each of us. Parental letters acknowledged our time for thanksgiving. Ever-present trials to probe and survive the pop quizzes regarding an equal doggedness of spirit arrived as well...

My dearest husband— A "brief" anniversary letter…

One week ago I thought I'd never write you, but I am so improved with everyone's concern that I am doing it…

This whole ordeal (severe, degenerative osteoporosis, and other complications) has bonded me close—with soul and body. We've always been as "one" with love and unity that is *so* rare…

I am so thankful you are successful with your "radiation seed" with prostrate surgery. Only my MAN would have the courage to gamble yourself to prolong a few more years…

My sudden spasm and fractured spine was a "shocker." We cried together once after the news and felt as a team, we could conquer—and *we shall*…

Our whole Xmas was united and super with family, but the arrival of "our PJ" was the brightest star of light and she has given so much of herself. We know—she *can* return…

A huge victory that our mutual love and spirit will survive. Our PJ is helping inspire me to do all this healing…

Our love has been cemented with love of family and concern, and that alone should make us get better the correct way. I adore you…

Feel my love and presence, especially to-nite as we are blessed with added company (our last born, PJ) on our 62nd anniversary…

I love you and every family member. We are a team unit almost unheard of in today's "mixed up world…"

I would marry you over and over—the perfect choice… My eternal love, Your Margaret

It was 2001. I paused for a hiatus. What made a splendid beeline straight to my heart was that my parents—valued friends for at least 50 years of my lifespan—took very little for granted. That dedicated consciousness and ultimate caring brought a potpourri of anticipation, joy, and wisdom to their union…

I shall always hold fast to my mindset that our world became a better-intentioned, kinder planet with their unselfish capacity and desire to "pay forward." Their chosen and earnest co-existence paved a pathway for other personas to shed their radiant light of being…

My conjecture? I was not biased, but savvy. My parents truly treasured humankind. Affirmative testimonials arrived yearly without my solicitation. I paid attention to close friends, acquaintances, and even strangers that expressed similar feelings about my parents. I read onward—in sync and proud with this shorter, humble note from JJ…

To My Treasure in Life and Living: You are *still* an unusual woman with many facets of living to be explored with you, Margaret…

I repeat—you are unique, still a challenging adventure—getting to know you…

Life is *never* a dull moment with you. We eagerly look forward to new adventures and accept the reverses as part of life's way…

My Dad's writing began to transition, particularly after their re-coveries from difficult surgeries. In hindsight, JJ kept visiting our town librarians to research—the talented surgeons with acclaimed outcomes...

I relived the reminiscences of JJ drawing pictures about her medical conditions and becoming overwhelmed with emotions. We cried together, a Dad and daughter in need of few words. I never knew exactly what JJ wrote to Madre during those transitional times—until this reading...

You are a determined fighter in life. I know in my heart everything will, in time, improve for you...

We are constant fighters in maintaining a union heading for the Century Goal, active, adventurous, and passionate...

Put it in high gear, honey! We're heading together, arm in arm, with a "halo" of love and desire not too many can match...

The twinkle and gleam the first Day I SAW YOU? I knew you and I belonged together...

Just be patient and firm as "you" march toward your goal to mend your physical problems. You are brave and determined, proving it can be DONE with faith itself, the medical staff, and the Good Lord or Spirit above...

We belong TOGETHER—THAT IS A PROVEN FACT—my beautiful, loving bride. I LOVE YOU! Your mate, John

I found myself rereading "...it can be DONE with faith itself..." and "...the Good Lord or Spirit above..." Their upbringing, denominations, and different choices were family stories long before this memoir...

My parents chose the Protestant denomination for our family. Madre was raised in the Episcopal church and a come-one, come-all small country church. JJ was raised Catholic by his Polish-Austrian, immigrant parents and became an altar boy...

JJ delved into and questioned his Catholic faith during college years—"after my philosophy of religion courses..." Dad's traversing, transformational sojourn was an understatement. "I was even agnostic for awhile..."

My mother had forged ahead with their quest to ascertain a denomination offering more breadth, leeway, or latitude. "Both of us yearned for something else, particularly for you girls as young, impressionable children..." There was a mutual decision that the Protestant faith could accommodate this initial, spiritual grounding. Later, as young adults, Madre and JJ enticed each of us to analyze religion, philosophy, and the art of critical thinking. We did just that ...

Undoubtedly, the ultimate pilgrimage came as no surprise. Throughout adolescence and adulthood, my parents elected to associate with people of diverse faiths. Whenever Madre and JJ brought us to visit their friends, each of us accepted at least one intention. Madre would declare, "Now, all of us will be attending their church denomination or synagogue not a Congregational church..."

I enveloped the telepathic messages that seemed to glide my way, akin to Scott Peck's—the road less traveled. Diversity was comfortable for my parents, a solace in their heart and wayfaring. They offered to serve as the regular hosts for our First Congregational church guests from intriguing countries and faiths...

Hindu faith, Buddhist beliefs, and vegetarian diets were presented to us ahead of today's world of diversity. Explore and inquire became our natural passages. Rereading letters, I kept noting "God...the good Lord above...have faith...a higher Spirit...on the other side—into eternity…souls growing together…" Now, I was witnessing the mirror likenesses in my training and rites of passage—Jitsu, Reiki-Shamballa, and metaphysical pathways…

Although one might have surmised that Christian faith was a worthy choice, there was another profoundness—the eclectic, inclusive spirituality that emanated from Madre and JJ. The wide-ranging exposure and divergent, religious beliefs resounded daily. Their daughters were destined to test and sift through future choices. Personally, I celebrated that my parents were open to "Namaste" in spite of the generation gap…

Namaste included subtle translations. Its universal "oneness" offered abundance in today's world of seeking, cultivating, upholding, and nurturing connections. I paused to refresh myself. Namaste—the shining light in me honors the shining light in you. Two—shining lights…

To my lovely wife and ETERNAL partner in 2002: The Good Lord directed my roaming eyes and heart to my Love in spite of my casual thoughts in college years of just a night out to enjoy dancing…

Today, as I look back each year on our special day, I thank my lucky stars that we met and married. I have no regrets…

Hope we are destined for the Century mark. I truly can say from the innermost depths of my heart, I look forward to them…

I know you are physically hampered in doing many things, BUT let me assure you I AM GLAD YOU'RE ALIVE and still moving physically…

In moderation, we shall still seek and enjoy adventurous trips that will not add stress and pain…

Hibernation at this stage of our physical life is STILL NOT WARRANTED; we have longevity on both sides of our family…

I say, "Let's do it sensibly while we can. You name it. We can DO IT…"

I LOVE YOU TO ETERNITY. ARE YOU WITH ME?…

Your Eternal lover, mate, and traveling PARTNER, John

Fascinating and rare—that my parents would compose the eloquent, riveting letters independently, yet ended up capitalizing or underscoring similar words and phrases…

Throughout the decades, I believed wholeheartedly that their testimonials, tributes, and positive regard for "individuality" reigned supreme. There was a mystical, prevalent grace in my parents' relationship of spirit and soul. One in another…

Madre penned these everlasting, spiritual memories. In 2002, the grace and serendipity continued—to a very special person—her John, Johnny, JJ…

My card to you about *souls* echoing and growing forever fits us perfectly…

We are blessed to have our daughter here to celebrate our anniversary…

You are the LOVE of my life…

So lucky to have you caring for me constantly and daily—no small task! I appreciate your patience and gentle caring for me day after day…

We surely have been on the same page—since we met 54 years ago…

I liked the prayer blessing for family that PJ gave us. Then Bev read at X-mas dinner…

Blessed with special people in our family. They all care and give of themselves constantly—such a devoted LOVE…

I truly believe our longevity comes from our deep love. Our lives are full to overflowing…

Our spirit and souls will always meet… Yours forever and ever, Marge

Perfect imperfections—I wrote that esoteric phrase in my books. I conveyed that truth-for-all during speaking engagements and creative prose venues. I upheld the authenticity of that enlightenment

as I sorted through the manila-clasped envelopes. This medley of letters casted a portrayal of Madre and JJ in a light of their perfect imperfections...

Madre scribed her letter—of these perfect imperfections—on their 66th Anniversary. It was 2003...

Dearest John—This has been a quite a year of struggles, but somehow we made it through many hard times. We'll march on to that drummer with a positive beat...

As you keep saying to me, "Think *positive!*" My love is that of your devoted wife and it encircles all my being, demands my most fervent prayers...

My reward is the *honor* of being your wife and Mother of all our *devoted* children and grandchildren...

Everyone gives their love to us *constantly* and shows their concerns for our health...

Many families today do not have that bonding of love. Somehow, our strong love got passed along to the next generation...

Our years have been endowed with faith, trust, and strong love...

Forever yours, Marge

Legacy and benevolence from generations...
Drummers march onward through strife and struggles...
Leaps of faith, entrustment, and conviction...

A Medley Of Inspiration
Birthday And Holiday Letters

I opened additional letters, the ones that Madre and JJ authored for birthdays and holidays. Reading this medley of compositions, a burst of inspirations came full circle.

The envelope that I pulled out was dated 1947. It contained a card and birthday letter scripted by Madre. John, Johnny, JJ—was back home safely from World War II...

Dearest John—Every year you become closer than the previous year, if that is at all possible... I can't begin to tell you how much I love and need you in my life...

Many times you are reading. I sit and gaze at you, wondering how I ever managed to get such a good-looking husband. I thought that way during this weekend. We had free time together—the first in a long time, sweetheart, now that you are back from WWII...

There is no other man in this world for me, even though we often joke about it! I am completely and utterly satisfied with our love and life...

When I question or nag a little about business, it is mostly because I am concerned about you and your future welfare—and, your hopes and dreams. I do want them all to come true...

May this, your 32nd birthday, bring you as much happiness and good wishes as anyone can possibly endow upon you...

You are the best husband any girl could ever desire. I feel strongly that we were just "mated" for one another...

All my love is yours—now and forever. Yours devotedly, Marge

Fast forward to 1952. Madre wrote JJ'S birthday letter on July 10th instead of the 25th. Well, she was due—pregnant with ME...

I never tired of hearing her spiel about big babe. "I was petite, but you were my biggest babe—almost nine pounds. My close friends had their babies. I was still walking the hospital corridors and visiting them that hot-sticky week. The whole month of July was unusually humid..."

I would tease my mother whenever the legendary tale was re-counted. "Hey Madre, I was your CANCER babe. As a devout water sign, I wanted to stay in YOUR beguiling womb..." And, of course, I managed to accomplish that feat (sic) for awhile...

Oh, I just knew. I developed a powerhouse—PJ's sense of humor in Madre's deep abyss. Just imagine—dramamine for her non-stop months of nausea and undoubtedly, my exotic and tidal dreamscapes...

Oh, I just felt certain. Madre's springboard-like, endless walk-abouts and that yucky castor oil that the docs kept dispensing? Why, the whole shebang only incarnated my ludicrous, side-splitting melo-dramas over the years...

The docs with their hopeful, enterprising endeavors "to try and induce labor" were routine for Madre's generation. Well, I finally ar-rived on the worldly scene. I heard this "big babe" received a splendid welcome—loving parents and in-a-tizzy sisters...

Their last-born PJ was predestined to become different. How could I not be, given my PJ take on birthing intentions from the womb? Hey, let's-put-it-off-for-awhile, ok Mom? No wonder Madre's cliffhanger story was chronicled time and time again. Apparently, I really flipped over my diapers-only existence that long, humid summer. Smitten, I was...

The next years of bliss with family outings became epic adventures. I was being toted, mesmerized, and played with EVERYWHERE that my parents and sisters traveled. These mini-dramas domineered and enhanced my stellar introduction to the cosmos...

As the last-born babe with older, on-the-fly sisters, I surprised and still managed to enthrall my parents. I stretched to keep pace with my sisters. Ah, the precocious child kept emerging and blossoming...

No great mystery why the youthful and adult years of where-was-PJ-going or what-was-PJ-doing quests and sojourns triumphed. I laughed aloud until I became fixated with Madre's next letter, feeling the tingles of anticipation and unvarnished truths...

I am having to write this before your actual birthday, John…

Many happy returns and I do love you very deeply. Still haven't had our fourth (first child was carried to term, but stillborn). Hope you will be happy—as happy as I—over its arrival…

Down deep inside, I realize this child has to be the last as far as age and finances go. You never made me feel our child had to be anything other than a healthy baby and for that, I thank you darling….

Madre's glowing revelations about not losing touch with cultivated values like quality time from business and their "special" letters touched a chord. She entrusted—there was "a simplicity" that spawned a richness for their life and love that few possessed...

My parents attended to "the moments." Family and significant others, new friends, adventures galore, and the spontaneity of living life to the brim struck the right rhythm and tempo. I fancied that Madre and JJ were fiesty spirits! Try and try again—not to take life and living for granted...

Even a short letter was touching, granting permission for the welling, gentle tear to drop down my cheekbone. Madre had tried—to stretch and blossom far beyond her youthful memories of loss. We, in turn, received and basked in the light of a resolute and less burdened woman for our mother...

When I watch you with our daughters, I know I lost something growing up...

But, we have quite a family now, John—our mutual efforts to overcome. All my love reaches out to you...

Can't you feel it, dearest John? Yours forever, Margaret

Early flashbacks were surfacing with this 1952 letter. JJ would be experiencing serious back surgery. By 1956, I was only four years old...

I visualized my recuperation images of JJ's bedridden year and his old-fashioned, cumbersome back brace. A year later, as a wee tyke of four years old, the warmth of our clasped-hand walkabouts in the mill town were mighty compelling. No matter what, I kept my promise to Madre. "NO! No, Daddy...this way!" Little PJ was not letting her Daddy take his mischievous turn—a short-cut walkabout for a yummy ice cream treat...

All of our family—tough cookies! Each of us managed to acquire immeasurable strength and hardy, survival-attitudes—whether conscious or subliminal...

To the most wonderful wife in the world: I am very happy to be your husband, celebrating this wonderful Christmas with our three offsprings. I sincerely hope the coming year will settle many things for us...

I only wish that I could do something unexpected for you someday soon, without the fear of disrupting our budget. I know you feel the same...

It feels much more valuable, this love of ours, as the years go by—to see it survive on the strength of mutual love and devotion…

Bless you my darling for all that you have done to make our marriage so happy. I am eternally grateful…

Merry Christmas, Margaret. I hope you are happy as I, your husband. Johnny

The year was 1963. It represented a challenging family time with mobility from a mill town to cosmopolitan and JJ's zip-to-the-top position with a new, corporate management. Plus the mini-tremors and mounting excitement of what the "unknowns" held in store…

My Dad was the top finalist. This leap-of-faith commitment and multi-faceted position meant the Herculean steps. All of us cheered for Dad—risk-take, wager, and tango on. The butterflies in our tummies were escalating for the right reasons. Voila! There would be newfangled beginnings and the re-inventions of who-knows-what…

Extreme pleasure to wish you Happy Birthday, Margaret for numerous reasons, but the purchase of our love nest means we are *completely* on our own…

I looked at cards and words were not suitable. I wanted down-to-earth expressions to tell you I would marry you again, without one moment of regret or hesitation…

Looking forward to the evenings of quiet interludes on our new porch. It is *really* good to live without the other burdens and restrictions of the past (ending our family business, decisions for the final sale, and garnering monies for my immigrant parents and their retirement)…

You deserve more praise and gratitude than the human pen can reveal on paper… Honestly and truthfully, I'm deeply grateful and indebted—your love and loyalty…

My need for you in the past and in the future has and will be great…

Without your love, courage, and faith in me, I may have hesitated to dig out. It takes a great partner to shape the future. That I have…

Am looking forward to our long future together… Yours forever, Johnny

JJ's poetic voice emerged again. The letter came with exquisite anecdotes for Madre's birthday in 1974...

To a wonderful wife who is always a radiant bride and truly needs no special days for isolated remembering, for each day is lit by her exuberance and love of life...

The people in Margaret's orbit are enriched every day by her voice, look, touch, and love...

You truly serve all—by your presence and loving devotions...

Fast forward to April 15, 1976. Years of letter writing had ensued across the last thirteen years. This time I pulled out and scanned a note to Madre...

My parents were colorful and articulate individuals. It came as no surprise to read "just a note"—not birthdays, anniversaries, or holidays. Just JJ's lively note and Robert Browning's eloquent verse...

It was a day of wonder and joy to receive your tender loving thoughts...

There is but one beautiful verse which would adequately sum up my own feelings...

I had to turn to Robert Browning—

Grow old along with me

The best is yet to be

The last of life for which the first was made.

No riches known to man can compare our love... With love everlasting, John

JJ composed a birthday letter that same year, 1976. It was characteristic of his poetic voice and talents. When he was in college, JJ pursued a double major—Business and English...

He yearned for the appealing footpath of becoming an English teacher. Those positions and limited money in Depression years thwarted his pilgrimage. However, the yearly birthday letters portrayed JJ's writing forte and star qualities. I was eager to return to my captivating moment—reading his fetching letter to Madre...

Dearest Wife and Adorable Mistress: May this birthday find your heart filled with untold happiness. It is an occasion for which I am most grateful…

You were brought forth as a being, just for me. For that, my gratitude and joys are boundless…

Treasures of the earth have been encompassed in our union, much of its immeasurable values due to you, your steadfast love, and your loyalty— unquestioned in the numerous vicissitudes of our life…

No living being could ask for more; you gave without a shadow of a doubt…

In giving, you have nurtured much happiness, not only to me and your family, but also to unnumbered people whose lives you touched, some briefly and others over a longer span…

None will consciously forget you and your graciousness, kindness, and unselfish love. Even in times of personal stresses, you obscured your pains. None knew your inner turmoils…

You gave strength and love without asking anything in return; a rare benevolence of inner quality few possess, never mind sharing without a moment of hesitation…

You took time for your own husband to love and learn, feeling the depths of your beautiful spirit, a firm and committed love…

Yes, I confess, it took time to quench my thirst from your well of giving and learn its full value…

Fortunately, I did not lose you in my blindness at times, for being just an unknowing man in such matters, I could have lost my greatest treasure of happiness…

Time and maturity, thank God for them, and the patience of a wonderful woman, but for her—I might never have had the riches I enjoy today and expect to enjoy for some time more…

Thank you—our wonderful family you gave us, your patient efforts, and time spent guiding their developments…

Though our daughters give us small hurts, being human with faults of their own, they are in total a mixed group of determined souls, taking qualities from both our sides. They meet the battles of this world with unflinching courage and fight…

In their struggles, I can see much of your work, strengths, and love guiding them thru the mazes of life…

It is no wonder, on this day, we all turn to you and express love and gratitudes…

So much debt owed to one lovely, unselfish, devoted being—YOU! Today, I ask and give in one breath, nothing tangible or materialistic of you…

May I have your undivided company for one whole day, just you and I holding hands, quietly loving and enjoying each other's company…

The day and eve will fill your memory book and your heart. A TICKET TO PARADISE…

There was a nirvana embodying their natural spirit. That paradise was the ultimate gift to us—their daughters—with no price tag. Quite simply, Madre and JJ strived to give unselfishly in any given moment of our upbringing…

At this stage of living, now in my late 60's, there was a genuine passion and sanctity to shadow their legacy. It was my endowment to savor and "pay forward" these unforeseen riches during my lifespan…

It was JJ's pen on-the-move-again in 1977. The loving wisdom was expressed as a holiday fortune…

Oh, how you have agonized, hinted, and threatened to invoke the "whole woman era" movement. Women do rule (men *really* know that)…

No male realizes the POWER OF WOMAN more than "I" after 40 years…

Like you have always hinted, it is the small things that count the most with women…

MERRY CHRISTMAS to all! May their fortunes be as GOOD… With LOVE, JJ

When the next year rolled around in 1978, it was Madre's pen-on-the-move that displayed a mutual Christmas rapture and unconditional caring. Her envelope displayed a glittery holiday seal and was entitled, "To my Perpetual Sweetheart, Merry Christmas!" Marge

Beautiful card on special people! My heart is full to overflowing with our love… Our love shows everywhere in us—our children—and yes, even our grandchildren…

I am one lucky woman. I count my blessings daily, not just holiday times, that I captured such a partner for my life fulfillment…

You give me the greatest gift of all—your steadfast LOVE… Thanks—for being you… Marge

By 1978, my Dad was retired. My proposed "PJ and Dad feat" was a piece of cake. I would tempt the gutsy, venturesome JJ—design a phenomenal, cross-country trip from Massachusetts to Ohio and then, tally ho—to our GRAND FINALE of Texas…

PJ's three conditions: be ingenious, be spontaneous, and arrive in the nick of time for my faculty meetings. PJ goodies included a winning invitation to hang out for a few weeks. Why not? Experience Texas exploits and greet my favorite colleagues at the university. Enjoy another PJ irresistible treat—a complimentary air flight home, jetting back to his esteemed Queen. Madre was not retired, but darn ready for the next dynamic-duo, Southwestern adventures…

Madre retired a few years later. My PJ promises of the royal, DOUBLE treatment came to fruition. "C'mon down, y'all…" In the interim, our captivating, 2,000-mile wayfaring included something else. Dad mailed the hilarious notes to Madre…

This Best Western letterhead comes from Pennsylvania and Kentucky. My Dearest Sweetheart: It was nice to chat briefly last night, but knew the youngest was eagerly waiting to talk, so I gave up my precious moments with you…

We had a *great* trip so far with weather very much in our favor. Though the mileage was heavy, it gave PJ more time at Columbus and Ohio State to expedite and investigate her inquiries…

After today, we shall move along with a bit of leisure and enjoy the scenes. Truly becoming amusing to find a place to eat, as all the wholesome places were closed on Sunday…

One place had LOUD MUSIC (disco style), you groped to find your way 'til the eyes became accustomed to semi-darkness. They were serving only in the lounge…

PJ didn't find atmosphere "enough of our adventuring…" so we departed to a Pizza Hut. We hope to experience more adventures plus a saner civilization. HA! We hope to hit upon Day's Inns until we arrive at Denton…

Miss you mucho even though I am enjoying talks and trip with PJ. Love Ya, John P. S. PJ adds, "Hi from me, too!" xoxo

My next letter comes from Kentucky. My Dearest! It was so good to hear your voice last night. Miss you plenty traveling for this period of time, for except in work, we have rarely been separated…

PJ appears to spring back after her two nights of deep discussions and book involvement… However, we hope to rest more leisurely the balance of the trip…

Hope to make a scenic stops, other than horse farms. Seeing the rolling hills of Kentucky are beautiful…

Glad you are busy with family and friends. Some places you would have enjoyed stopping and spending a day, particularly with your painter's eye! Miss you…

Next destiny was our fabulous touchdown at "my digs" in Denton, Texas. JJ was a daily scribe, enlightening his darling. I kicked up things a few notches. Yep, the PJ crackerjack of home-turf surprises was on a roll. Pardon, what an understatement. JJ was thrilled on a daily basis! It was no coincidence. My colleagues and new friends adored JJ…

Miss you more and more—life with this time gap without Margaret is tough…

Texas is filled with new sights, but nothing can truly take your place…

Casey, the gentleman she has been dating, has been lucky. He got tickets for a Cowboy's game and rodeo. He hopes to accomplish the same for you when we come down…

We are staying over his place to see Trader's Village. In Denton, everyone is anxious to meet you from her faculty and want us at their homes…

They all enjoy PJ—her abilities and accomplishments. You'll also love the shops in western style downtown…

Eating places are intriguing and tasty to say the least. It'll be difficult to control the waistline…

PJ is treating me with specials at home along with treats outside…

Texas is VAST and we will have to plan well…

I try to give PJ and Casey time together. It gives me time to write you. I am extremely proud to be your husband and lover…

PJ brought your letter, upon returning from office. All of us had good laughs with your card. I am eager to see you, love…

Retirement years were forthcoming. Madre earned and deserved the best, just like JJ. My primary wish was that they maintained their good health to experience and luxuriate with the impromptu Texas and New Mexico adventures and our quality time…

My own phrase—Attitude = Altitude—fired into high gear. My PJ heart-chakra was oscillating. Beautiful karma! My parents' unconditional love and deserving joy could and would evolve…

This year's birthday in 1981 was such a warm one with anticipation of our retirement years, a very mutual one, John…

I, too, have the "gut feeling" that God will grant us this very enjoyable time of our lives. Thank you for asking me to marry you and giving me so much happiness along the way…

Some things never change with time—children still go barefoot, jonquils grow in spring, babies still reach upward to adults, meadowlarks still sing, and heavenly stars still shine above…

The world has more need of gentle hearts and love that is warm and true like yours. Your thoughtful deeds make the world a better place with your kindness…

Your ever-giving love to me, our children, and now, our grandchildren will always bring you joy the whole year through, not just for one day…

You give your children advice, but also know they need to think things out for themselves and form their own conclusions…

Emerson said, "Though we travel the world over to find the beautiful, we must carry it with us or we find it not." How true and this applies to you, John, with your giving…

So happy that I can be with you on your 66th… Yours forever, Marge

It was 1983. Madre's outlook in JJ's 68th birthday letter reflected her deep-rooted attitude of gratitude, affinity, and sustenance. As a Reiki master, I felt her gentle cadence and the vibrations. My parents wrote the rhetoric of serendipity and solace. They sought karma and soul-filled revelations on a daily basis. How fortuitous—Madre and JJ embraced that essence ahead of the Zen, Jitsu, and Reiki paths of today…

….all the best with health. I shall pray that I regain my full health and be around to enjoy the "twilight years" with you…

Robert Browning once said, "Take away LOVE and our Earth is a tomb." Our love has no decay; we hold onto our yesterdays, todays, and all the tomorrows…

Memories make an everlasting love like a stream that flows forever—without a pause…

This year was difficult for us and *you were the one* who pulled me through grief…

You have taken my hand more than once over the period of years and led me through the showers that brought sunshine…

Your love, sympathy, understanding, and sharing of pain sustained me through my serious surgery…

Sometimes, I worry about our deep love and that you seem to make your life around me—and then, I find myself doing the same thing…

Love was there the day we met, strong and enduring. Our lives came together, blending in an assured tranquility…

Our spirits met on that golden, September day with our first kiss—leaving us speechless…

I recall the greeting and spirits meeting as we hung in space, two souls blending with one single thought—our love and unity, as our hearts beat as one…

When day is done, I have been so comfortable with you…

…our big love that many people never feel or experience. Sleep settles quickly, like a quilt wrapped about my body…

We two—in silence—become as one again, on this your 68th year…

Each year becomes more precious as time marches onward, my first and only man in my heart and life…

Our caring keeps me warm, at peace with the world, alive and young at heart…

Fast forward… JJ continued the themes of adjustments, balancing, and setbacks to Madre on her birthday in 1994. Rereading, I appreciated their abundance—of honoring one another…

We've had adjustments to each other, two strong and loving personalities working together to make a home, family, and a worthy, successful union…

Struggles and setbacks—but we loved, worked together, and today, we have a loving family and life together…

I honor you today, grateful that fate brought us together. Looking back, we dared and achieved much. I think, even in these times, we would have made the grade…

I admire the unique, fascinating woman you have become—regal and gracious in stature, yet wearing a touch of compassion and understanding when mingling with humanity…

The road ahead is still very long, and like Frost stated, we will travel the path others do not —thus, filling our life together abundantly…

Look ahead with me—joyful adventures to be tasted. They are beckoning us…

I love you, Marge for eternity…

Madre affirmed JJ's musings and homage expressed in 1994. These reflective intentions encapsulated their unity, peace, and a meditative spirit of enlightenment. The reciprocal feelings and kinship came "full circle" to JJ on his birthday...

May your day be full of happiness. We are blessed at this stage—we share contentment, fun, and keep beauty in our everyday living, something money cannot purchase...

I see discontentment about us many times and marvel at our 56 years together...

We had our struggles, but they served to enhance our good years...

We support one another constantly and that is why our marriage ties are so strong...

Even our grandchildren picked out a card this year, thanking you for your guidance and wisdom. They show us their steadfast love...

Our daughters—all different, but most important all caring. Just as PJ and Casey sent you on Father's Day—"you are a guiding light"...

You have been a caring husband, parent to your children, and beyond that, you gave a great deal of love to your parents. I love you deeply for all you gave to them—lucky people to have you as their *son*...

We have lovely children, all beautiful because they were "love babies!" All love...

In closing, you are my #1 in my book forever. It is why I've enclosed a poem on "we are one..."

When you blow out the candles, I know you are counting all blessings. We are *one*—always...

The manila-clasped folders held another gratuity, a fringe benefit for my evolution. I extracted the PJ letters that I had composed throughout the years...

I pulled out a birthday essence scribed to JJ in 1994. The past, present, and future were melding. I voiced how familial qualities had been carried purposefully into my contemporary passages. I was living away from New England, pursuing my academic career...

I missed "being there" on JJ's special day, but took advantage of my semester breaks. I chose purposefully again, teaching only part-time in the summer. Once I could afford it, I elected not to teach any of the summer terms...

There was ownership of my passion—to soar back home for unforgettable visits, esteemed connections, indelible nudges, and the imprints left upon my heart. These breaks manifested the sublime awakenings—for my students and myself...

I ascended to become a more innovative professor, writer, and mentor. A partnership of these roles and a skyrocketing energy to greet each academic year morphed into something else. I was compelled with a novel spirit. I wanted to explore the intimate process of knowing and not knowing...

My commitment ensured purposeful opportunities and choices. Outside of my unforeseen time with serious health scenarios, I honored the PJ self-promises. No regrets...

When I was unable to travel, I adopted the PJ Plan A. That plan was part of my daily reminders—the near-future trips to my parents, sisters, and a beloved New England homestead. In the interim, there was PJ Plan B. My special letters and free spirit would still come forth in special letters...

Dearest JJ— A Happy Birthday across the miles! Darn, I can't have our plane fixed to be there (I wish!). This letter is one for a memory lane, but an encouragement to continue your antics into the future. What am I referring to…

Your sense of humor. Why yes, I am *encouraging* you to stick to your beliefs on this day and always. All of our family times with travels and picnics included magnifico adventures, being lost (a lot!), antics, and a sprinkling of laughter…

Vacations at Lake Winnepausakee were the epitome of this combo. Perhaps, that's an understatement…

With Texas adventures, there is frolic, play, and laughs (get lost a lot!). That combination adds zest to our relationship, love, and continues to keep perspective on reality—a much-needed "balance" in life...

I'm amazed at how often I relearn these lessons. Or even find scenarios to entice such a momentum. I am convinced—I garnered your deviant genes. Ha…

As I teach over the years, these qualities are what takes my students off-guard, but they become our connecting force—kindred spirits, you might say…

There are days as I reflect upon family gatherings or recent visits. I see your presence—playful, sensitive, and genuinely aware of life's offerings. So today, I toast and cheer those images that I can easily recreate…

And, I thank *you* for showing me *how* that's done for a lifetime! You let me venture forth with that same spirit coupled with a PJ-blend and persona…

JJ, you have shared and enticed those wondrous traits. Always your #3 Weirdo, Yank-Tex, PJ Mucho love xoxo

The same year, my eldest-sister Patti Jo, casted her spellbinding, intuitive insights to JJ. She elaborated upon a treasure trove of memories. I became engrossed and rapt with attention as that letter was pulled from a manila-clasped folder...

I still missed Patti Jo's teary-eyed dabbling that came with top-shelf laughter and a fog-horn style of nose-blowing. Recreating vibrant images of her petite stature was easy. Wee Patti Jo fitted splendidly under my PJ-armpit! I often swept my far-reaching arms and hands 'round her Lilliputian being...

Lilliputian sister fitting perfectly...

Rapt with sisterly rapport and simpatico caregiving...

Sisterhood expanding, tranquility to their souls...

She had passed away unexpectedly—horrific, pancreatic cancer in 2005. In a mystical way, Patti Jo's celestial spirit was comforting and revitalized our sisterhood bonds. I chose to linger and reread her softhearted, insipid excerpts...

Dearest Dad— Happiest Birthday to you. May your next year be a wonderful one, full of treasured memories. I hope this is the year that you win the big lotto. Anyone who studies and tries so hard deserves to win…

The older I get and listen to others, the more fortunate I feel to have the basic foundation that you created for our family…

Thank you for being the father that took time out to play with us…

I can't even count all the places we've gone as a family and the fun we've had. The enjoyment of "adventures," learning history, and a love of nature…

Thank you for the years that you included Nana and Grandpa on our day trips. Family memories are stored up in the heart, bringing joy in my life…

Thank you for all the laughter you have brought to my life…

Your sense of humor keeps us happy. Sometimes in my teens, I cringed at your teasing. Then I saw how my friends reacted and wanted to come to my house….

You became the father no other kids had and I was proud, bragged a lot…

Thank you for your patience and understanding…

We're different daughters, yet you treat us the same with fatherly love and guidance, allowing us to be ourselves. Thank you for that most precious treasure…

Time was zipping along. I opened a Mother's day letter dated 1995. It was chock full of JJ's stunning recognition of Madre—as an admirable woman, wife, and mother...

To a beautiful wife and mother— I gaze and wonder "HOW" I managed to win and hold your love over these years. There are many facets to your total image as woman, mother, and wife…

You truly deserve and have earned an Honorary Degree of Doctor in many phases and facets of life, confronting challenges with intelligence and understanding, yet always with a deep touch of love and motivation…

You have touched the life of many individuals. One can see positive responses, derived pleasure, and pride in the eyes of those favored by your friendship…

I have stated many times, they destroyed the "mold"—that is *why* there is only "ONE OF YOU"… Love you and thank "you" for saying, "Yes! Yes!" John

That same year, Madre reciprocated—noting JJ's luminous being and attributes. Her wedded bliss was intentional…

Life would be empty without you, so let's march forward to another decade, God willing…

I reflect about our youth. We had lots of dreams and aspirations—and somehow, along the way, we overcame defeats and came out triumphant in our 57 years of wedded bliss…

We accomplished a wonderful family of lovely, caring daughters. Without you, I could not have completed this overall picture of close family life…

We have grandchildren who care and son-in laws that are enjoyable. Many people aren't this lucky. I am yours to eternity…

Madre finished with a poem that denoted a metaphorical comfort, likened to a deep sleep or relaxing, fireside glow. There were expressions of sensitive feelings—like those conjured up with melodic music and the onset of spring. And, of course, a myriad of manifestations with her abiding, unconditional affections…

That summer of 1995, I was destined to read a particular birthday letter. Patti Jo was in Texas, a first "how-y'all-doing visit!" To be far away from New England on JJ's birthday was another "first tale" and unique exposure…

I already sensed a balance act—tentativeness and perpetual excitement—with a new region, southwestern culture, and a handful of

the "never-witnessed" realities. Alas, Patti Jo would share her tender overture before the royal send-off from Texas...

A first—writing you from miles away in Texas, but at PJ's little farm in the countryside brings us closer—a New England treasure, just like you...

Feels funny—not to be celebrating on your day at home with all the gang...

Thank you for being the loving, compassionate, protective Dad you are. I'm fortunate to have that in a father. The blessing of having that is hard to express...

But we daughters know it, feel it, and that's what counts...

Thanks for working hard during all our growing-up years at home, taking time to make a house a *home*, and be what a father is *meant* to be...

I'm proud to say, "my Dad" and be able to mean all that entails. Missing you from this vast and different Tex land... Have a wonderful day. Love ya!

Patti Jo was also starting a chapbook, requesting my mentorship along with her promenade of discovery learning. I cultivated our defining junctures and rites of passage, whether in Texas or back home...

I upheld our "Karr" tradition to script the letters—my birthday and keep-in-touch notes. Patti Jo's chapbook, Under His Wings, was finally on its way. She claimed, "I am sending my chapbook Godspeed to my towering, lanky, and funny Yank-Tex sis..."

Rereading this Texas birthday letter to JJ was omniscient. It was uplifting in today's superlative moments. No coincidence. Another celestial bestowal would crop up shortly thereafter...

I pulled gently from a manila-clasped folder, receiving a 1995 birthday letter written by whom? No one else...of course, JJ. His letter disclosed a stalwart spirit and enamored intentions to adorn and enliven his sweetheart...

To my wife, lover, and inspirational spirit—for our wonderful life together...

This letter is a call for planning excursions together over the summer and fall…

We still have the energy and abilities to savor adventures together, pointing the car in any direction, enjoying the blessings of being together…

You remain an exciting woman and a very big "joy" in my life…

I truly needed "you" in my life and faith…

Luck and compatible vibes blended us for life together to "Eternity!" I can readily see why our children and grandchildren love you dearly…

You personify the image of loving, a woman who gives much of herself without demanding anything in return…

The world should literally be peopled with individuals of your disposition and character, male and female…

It wouldn't be in the Hellish mess of today's times. I love you, Sweetheart

I noted the impeccable timing—it was Father's day, 1995. Madre's dynamic, rousing messages were cathartic. Undoubtedly, they became ardent intentions for her special John, Johnny, JJ…

Dearest John: Just a note to tell you in my book—you are an *exceptional* Dad… You gave of yourself at any early age to *each daughter* in a special way…

I hear from all of them (and, it is mutual). "We have the best Dad. We were lucky." Not all luck. Lots of patience, caring, and giving of oneself…

You have that knack of relating the right way, even through our rough times…

The road to happiness is never smooth one, *but* we certainly formed a strong love that bonded all of us, something all the lotteries in the world could not purchase…

We were meant to live and cherish one another. The Lord has blessed us with unusual love…

My whole life is *peaceful* with you by my side. I am yours forever—Margaret

I reached for another letter, noting the date of July 25, 1995. How languishing to discover my own musings, a maturing journey expressed to JJ on his birthday. I was heralding our kindred spirit across

the 2,000 miles and an overlap of new challenges amidst family roots and wings...

Feel my spirit and well wishes across the miles on your birthday! To live life, only with serious intents and little enjoyment or laughter is limiting. Thank you for our family roots and wings... With the spontaneous joys and laughter, there can be enlightenments and wisdom. Thank you for our family roots and wings...

It is a delicate balancing and blend—a "go-getter" spirit, challenges, dreams, laughs, and pleasures—to capture a fuller picture of life and living. Thank you for our family roots and wings...

Your role-modeling and philosophy afforded insights to enhance my journeys and choices. Student evaluations for decades also endorsed my avid pursuit of authentic teaching-learning styles, enthusiasm, humor, perceptiveness, and nurturing...

I knew, even with the "individual PJ style and flair," that I learned these appealing roots and wings earlier in life with an exciting, enthusiastic Dad...

Your actions *and* words were a match! As I matured and saw people who concentrated on problems and created stressors by their choices, I reaffirmed the worth of early family lessons... Such a joy—to keep trying to develop. None of us has a crystal ball (I wouldn't want one)... Due to your positive influences coupled with PJ endeavors, I forged ahead with determination and humor. Thank you for these roots and wings. I gathered intangible riches for my journeys ahead. For your unselfish sharing and actions, I can never express enough thanks... I love you!

JJ's spunky attitude, passion for enrichment, and lifetime stretches to learn were visible, clear as a crystal gem. What a marvel to read another letter about the "courtship" vibes between my parents. A witnessing of their arresting relationship became a phenomenal legacy...

I reread the letter that captured a winter wonderland and their limitless love. It was 1995 and another Valentine's Day to manifest a full-Monty tribute...

Darling, 58 years ago I was excited dating you…

Today, that feeling has nurtured itself beyond descriptive words—I LOVE YOU… My steady girl grew to a woman, enriching my life beyond my limited abilities to put into words…

Yes, this is a small tribute along with our twosome dinner to the most wonderful woman in the world. You have given much of yourself to me and your family…

Your contribution cannot be measured in monetary forms…

In spite of our setbacks of varied sorts, we are enjoying a wonderful, rich life…

Yesterday, I did not know as a youth, but today as I look back, you have made life very rich in innumerable ways…

Please stay determined and healthy for many loving years… Always in love with "You!" John

Madre's letter personified a daily tenacity, a mutual commitment to sustain the magic and vitality of love. It was 1996 and another birthday celebration for her JJ, Johnny, John…

Dearest John— Life brings many changes, but the things that really count are those we can rely on—things like your thoughtfulness, your warm and caring ways, and all the special LOVE that you show daily…

I truly believe our strong love gives us the strengths that keep us alive…

You are there—understanding. You give a "magic" meaning to love…

There were additional revelations—about intimate, private times and splurges. In spite of Madre's frugal, Scottish background, both of them ventured to their first beacon of light—Hanover, New Hampshire. Their cups runneth over with countless, courtship memories…

My parents yearned to travel "ahead of the girls and grand-children…" They even rearranged a job consult in northern New Hampshire timed in accord with JJ's actual birthday. However, they never strayed far from the familial love and appreciation. Madre's letter ensued…

We have true family love, John. Three wonderful, caring daughters and compassionate son in-laws fill our world. We are blessed on your 81st year... Forever & Always, "Your Margaret"

After untold years of a finespun balance of individuality and consensus, there was Madre's astute closure. She believed wholeheartedly in their manifestations of choice, harmony, and a positive life force. One year later in 1996, these parallel themes reappeared. JJ heralded their consummate, refined balance in his celebratory tribute of Mother's day...

Darling—just a small token of tribute to you as a mother of our fine children. That is a solid, broadside compliment in my humble opinion—regal motherhood...

You do care in-depth about your children—yesterday, today, and the tomorrows not yet evident...

I can never fully express my intense love, caring, and concern for you...

This world has changed drastically in spite of the caring individuals who see the changes...

People can't understand the "how" and "why" WWII happened in our lifetime, in spite of human sacrifices of lives to improve life worldwide...

Yet, we can matter—in the choices and directions of our lives. You have stressed and shown that it can be done, if love and cooperation are solid in the union of two individuals who care enough for each other, plus the family they create...

If the same strengths and desires are held and improved upon, life will survive... It is seen in the efforts our children put forth in their lives and aspirations, due in great part to your guidance...

You were the constant image by their side expressing and guiding our visions, hopes, and dreams for their lives to be blessed with their hopes and dreams...

In my mind's eye, you have done an extraordinary work of *living art* with our children...

We, somehow, endured and conquered many obstacles along the way to achieve our well-earned happiness and love...

I know you feel the joys and the warmth of love from our children and family—You GLOW!

You are a Beacon, like the sailor's lighthouses guiding them away from dangers…

I could go on, but you want me to stop, for your crown is unsteady due to swelling! Honestly,

I believe you can still take more and keep a regal poise…

You enjoy every minute, as you have earned and deserve it. The finished canvas is always

getting a "touch-up" here and there…

A true artist—your brush is NEVER STILL! Love ya, Darling. See you soon on our date!

It was 1996. Given my serious health conditions coupled with an unmistakable PJ-grit and self-confidence to heal, it was no mystery. Madre agreed right away. She hand-wrote my slurred, slow dictation of a birthday letter to JJ…

Madre was observant—my esteemed mother—a stalwart caregiver, steady nurturer, and everlasting friend. Everyone concurred about why she bolted ASAP to Texas…

Madre was present for the revered moments of family advocacy and lending a spiritual consciousness to my healing process. She grasped the generosity and healing balm of our attachments. Carpe Diem! Yes, both of us seized the moments of rare connection to a higher source and well being. Madre began my letter with a prelude…

PJ, the composer and Madre, the script writer…

A happy, belated birthday from Texas, JJ! As we celebrate your birthday, I cheer you onward to your favorite—126 years young…

Throughout my relapses and recovery, I give credence and credit— my genes are inherited psychologically, not just physically…

I hear your words, but also feel them in my heart and soul. "Hang tough, PJ! Keep trying to figure out what works, analyze, discard, and keep the best. Set visions—perhaps a new life style, balance, and Casey by my side…"

Hard for me to write a check (sic). See my PJ teasing-smile, happy face…

Your birthday gift is $$—for Powerball and a must-do treat at your favorite Dairy Queen with

Madre. Walmart for another fix—snicker bars? Mucho love

Madre penned JJ's 1996 birthday letter as I wished—on my luminous card with two parakeets. Writing this Spellbound memoir, I came across my card in a manila-clasped folder. It was shouting (sic) from the back of my bedroom closet…

I paused wittingly. I reread this glossy parakeet card and my messages, twenty-two years later on June 4, 2018…

I abandoned the Spellbound writing that day to luxuriate and relish the soul-filled readings. I gazed at my colorful card, appreciating that Madre had scripted the 1996 letter, but not all of the reasons "why" she was caregiving…

On June 5th, the next day, I envisioned the lustrous parakeet card and my messages. I began anew—refreshed with a quintessential day of PJ compositions for this Spellbound memoir…

Fast forward… After his death in 2011, JJ kept sending me the signs—multipliers of five, mainly fifteen—often an abundance of nickels or shiny pennies. He loved coins and my birthday—July 15th. So I chose to kibbutz and felt "at peace" with his next signs…

JJ's silhouette facial signs—the distinctive youthful or elder imagery—came forth within the cumulus clouds. Just ask. Another day, I detected $15.00 in a meaningful locale with a significant other. Later that evening, his facial image appeared in the moon, like an old photo…

No coincidence—a meditative-like stillness happened whenever I yearned for his support or heartfelt presence. No wonder my 1996

letter, prodigious recollections of JJ's advice about my health relapses and healing process, began to echo again...

I sensed JJ's telepathic presence, and now, a similar Madre omnipresence. I accepted my Dad, the intuitive and savvy JJ, as a forever-friend and an earth angel. Now, as my guardian angel, JJ's words of advice were hovering and flittering, just like my PJ dance spirit. There was an acceptance of this realm—just knowing. Plus, a firm mindset that there was no such thing as no coincidence...

That same week, there was a mini-reunion of my health remnants. Stop, wait patiently, and watch for the Godspeed presence or images of my parents...

My eyes brimmed with tears. I took deliberate, strong-willed breaths. My heart-soul messages of love, everlasting gratitude, and AHA moments surrounding a prodigious grace emerged...

That day, I cruised to a favorite locale to write the Spellbound memoir. I brought three gems—my two parakeets card, healing messages, and my never-on-sale "MK" watch. I gazed at the rose-gold watch and recalled her artwork signed MK. Past images of Madre as PJ's scribe for JJ's birthday letter and caregiver in Texas rebounded. Yesterday's mini-reunion with health remnants? Gone! Nowadays, I evoked my healing paths, Jitsu, and Reiki-Shamballa training...

Just ask, discard, and release what was no longer mine. Manifest my intentions. My PJ health remnants were waning...

The two parakeets card was placed back gently into my bling "Hollywood" pocketbook. The design showed "JK" as the director for "Scene 7" and a woman—who looked like my twin. I smiled...

Of course, JK—John Karr! PJ exemplified the actress for Scene 7, my favorite number since childhood. Deep sighs and tranquilly that eve dignified my parents' tithe beyond measure. An attitude of gratitude appeared in a flash...

More gifts, please—from the manila-clasped folders. Madre had penned a Father's day mini-memoir in 1996. The envelope read, "You are the Greatest Dad Ever!" Read onward, PJ...

Dearest Husband— I can't begin to match your "Regal Motherhood" letter to me on Mom's Day. I treasure your thoughts...

We were meant to be as "one" and God is granting us long, twilight years...

Deep down, I feel our intense love over the years through happiness and struggles has sustained us and prolonged our lives...

We are at peace with one another and bask in our strong ties of love. Daily, we are there for one another...

I know I don't have to run out and get some material gift to let you know you are a *terrific* Dad to our girls and our grandchildren, who hold you in high esteem... You are an unusual man, always giving of yourself to me and others...

Everyone turns to you for advice in some form or another. I am sorry that we have one daughter really in a health struggle...

PJ is too young. I pray for answers daily...

This year, our trip to Texas will be a difficult one to see her and realize in person what she has to endure...

PJ has "guts." We can all try to give her *hope* every day—and count our blessings that we can make the trip at our age to help her heal. She needs us to endure....

I talked to our mutual friend, John, the other day and shared my fear. "I've lost one daughter. I *don't* want to lose another..."

We don't have to recapture a strong love. We just have to enjoy our good luck at meeting 58 years ago—being happy, even in war years, and becoming *closer* with each passing year… You are the one *and* only Man in my life. Keep "pouring love" my way… Yours, Marge

Alas, JJ's speedy reply—an empathic note to bolster Madre's spirit regarding my serious health scenarios. This note depicted his bold, handwritten style. The envelope made me crack-up immediately—1996 IMMEDIATE Air Express! Undoubtedly, it was Madre's fun-lovin' and perceptive JJ…

To My Wonder Woman: I am writing Very Early this Year—To keep your spirits, love, and enthusiasm HIGH during this Holiday Season, given the prevailing circumstances of our youngest daughter, PJ…

Your Very Supportive Husband, Lover, and Closest FRIEND, CONFIDANT, under ALL CIRCUMSTANCES…

My parents were definitely "on the same page." It was not a trite remark or today's buzzwords. Their durable, unwavering connections during my unpredictable health ordeals and doctors' dire forecasts were incredible. Nowadays, I revisited the opportune moments to assimilate my healing process throughout the years…

The past decade-plus, I cultivated an inner stillness with consistent meditations and journaling, practiced Kundalini yoga, and pursued Reiki-Shamballa training. The sensation of my parents' presence or signs became a viable, healing balm. This higher consciousness was a comforting support and a karmic vibration. No illusions… I was catching the esoteric drift of pure truths…

Another deep-rooted, cosmic vibration came forth. I relived what my older sister had offered to share—a Patti Jo birthday letter to Dad, composed in 1996…

As I reread, there were instants to dwell longer and discern the valued flashbacks. Truths became transparent. I was deeply moved. Patti Jo's reminiscences and blessings enfolded me in a golden aura of complete gratitude…

…May your day be "special" at the lake, our old place of wonderful memories as a family. Dad, your planning was *always* the greatest…

Thank you for giving us learning, fun times, and building our sense of wonder and seeking. You are a special father and I am blessed…

…making a home where all our dreams could be born and grow, nourished by your love. It was a place where we could come back for rest and peace, even today, in the midst of our struggles…

Even when you can't solve a problem, just being there for us makes a difference…

May God's love save and keep you eternally. Love always

Fast forward to the years of 1997 and 1998. JJ was on-a-classic-roll with Madre birthdays. My dearest Bride and Queen became her nick-names over a few decades. And, no surprise—JJ became the Prince. In hindsight, I qualified this entitlement—the zealous, true-blue Prince of Charm (sic)…

At the tender age of 18, as our grandson would put it—your 81st birthday—I'd like to invite you for a drive into southern New Hampshire and dinner…

I don't plan to climb a cliff for flowers or evergreens. Don't toss in your sleep trying to guess. You will *enjoy* the day… Thank you for being my BRIDE…

I hope to live with you as long as breath and body will allow us… Are you READY? I love you, John

"You" still are a very individualistic mold of a QUEEN. As a couple of determined people, still madly in love with each other, we will celebrate 60 years of wedded bliss and bonding with the Big D…

We've had close calls with our "Maker," yet we turned down the call and continued to add a little record for ourselves...

Shall we try for a dual 70th, and then proceed with these giant steps—onward to startle the nation? Somehow, by a quirk of fate, we have been determined to push on, overriding pain and tough times, and enjoying adventures together...

I guess we inspire each other with love and working out mutual decisions of life and living...

Somehow, I love meeting new challenges with "you" by my side...

We kick things around in our peculiar fashion and results come together... Logic, it may not be, but it miraculously comes out. You hesitate, BUT force yourself into action, positive results...

Is that the mystery of our attraction? It must be a strong, new glue—it works...

Enjoy your parties. You've earned every one of them, my Grand Lady...

I love you—lifelong... Happiness from your PRINCE, John

Queen Madre adored the legacy of her letters to Prince JJ. This particular day of writing, I came upon a special letter for Father's day. It was dated 1998...

What a premier bestowal—Madre's letter sketched the stellar breadth and depth of father-daughter relationships. I sat in stillness—for who-knows-how-long. I soaked in their life compass that exposed the compassionate and esoteric imprinting of courage...

Dearest John— Just a note to let you know I think you are the best father my girls could have wished for. It is easy to see they worship you and cling to every bit of your perceptive advice...

You have a close-knit love because that is what you gave them from birth. Patti still treasures and rereads her V-J letters, no doubt the one who recalls the World War II the most. Beverley comes home to share...

PJ waited for our trip to Texas for encouragement—her serious health problems. PJ truly knows all the pain you have endured with courage....

You are a shining example to bestow courage upon others. Thank you for being my friend,

lover, husband—always there for me…

You are truly an exception to the rule…

We tangle once in awhile, but it does not last long. Let's face it, we live together 24 hours a

day with harmony…

I know I am a very happy woman because I have YOU…

I shall love you forever and ever. Yours, Marge

Fast forward to 1999. Why, I found a lovely, colorful letter—on Valentine's Day. JJ had illustrated a fun-loving card, portraying a colossal heart with arrows and a Cupid for his Queen Madre…

Sweetheart, you pierced my Heart years ago. Today, I offer nourishment—Russell candies—to

nurture anew…

Bless you always for your steadfast love and support. Eternally yours…

No computer BUGS! This is a firm note of my love…

Will you celebrate our love this Valentine's Day? Dinner together! You pick place, time, and,

of course, I am included in the package with you…

I await your command, my Queen…

The Chariot is READY! Your lover, husband, and hopefully, the Man of your Life.

Please say, "YES!"

She accepted the invitation and flew yonder in a gilded-gold Chariot. Alas, Queen Madre and Prince JJ. That same year, Madre underscored the struggles, blessings, and a heightened awareness of options, free will, and living their dreams…

You and I are going to greet the year 2000, so how blessed can we become? Somehow, in

spite of struggles along the way, we have reached the *height* in our love and compassion for

life along with our wonderful children…

Many couples do not reach our plateau…

After the family 84ᵗʰ birthday celebration, we could take a ride on Sunday to Cock' N Kettle and detour home via Powerball. Being your birthday, we just might win something? Your choice!

Like Eckert Tolle, Madre and JJ made a decisive call. Their desire and capacity to exemplify and personify the "now" in their treks of seeking truths, allegiance, and hope were clear as a bell...

JJ's unexpected surgery and a loving son in-law with health issues kept the now-focus on their front burner. Their willful hopes and advocacy with my PJ bravado, steadfast conviction, and recurrent healing process underscored Madre and JJ's fearless capacity to welcome the "now"...

We share mutual worries and hope—that our PJ will continue to climb the *hard roads* to recovery...

Families are hidden treasures, so we must continue to seek them and enjoy all the riches...

I read that character contributes to beauty—it has helped fortify me in these times of family health concerns...

You, too, have a certain mode of conduct, a standard of courage, fortitude, and integrity. I keep saying you, John, are one in a million...

Madre ended the last part of a tender letter with an Anne Campbell poem. The poetry was symbolic, a glowing affirmation. It was not the greeting, not the kiss...

It was the choice—to let their spirits intertwine and meld. That classic, spellbinding realm was reinforced as I selected another note to read—JJ to Madre on Mother's Day. It was 1999, a hallmark year of the gestalts—when the quintessential "light bulbs" came on...

...this morning, as I kept glancing at you out of the corner of my eyes, EVERYTHING came into focus. So-o-o simple...

Yes, a dictionary of reactions, feelings, and expressions from—Just a Box of WHITMAN'S

Chocolate Sampler…

YOU ARE FAR MORE VALUABLE than any material matter…

I LOVE "YOU" to ETERNITY!

Shortly thereafter, JJ scripted another love note. He took care to acknowledge the span of years in concert with a quality time together…

2/14/1939–2/14/1999: 60 years! JJ exhibited more loving-kindness as he entitled the charismatic prose. THE LETTER of all letters—to HIS QUEEN—no matter what life and living tossed their way…

SWEETHEART …

You Pierced my Heart

Years Ago

Today I offer You

Sweet Nourishment

To Nurture Your Passions Anew!

It is 2001. To the Dearest and Most Precious Woman in MY LIFE!

Age—those advancing years—do not accelerate the faculties of the Mind, Body, and Spirit

on endearing and tender matters…

I NEVER anticipated in futuristic thoughts seeing "you" the MOST PRECIOUS woman in

my LIFE so limited in physical activities…

I envisioned AGE—YES— but with your absolute, normal motions. I saw a lovely, becoming

lady of Grace and Beauty still fascinating and strutting about, planning adventures together…

I quietly weep in my sleep or even waking hours, and wish I or someone skilled could improve

your physical abilities to enjoy and appreciate more physical motion…

Yet, I am eternally and deeply grateful that we are still enjoying a loving life TOGETHER…

If I could transfer some of my physical abilities, I would gladly share them with "YOU"—the

MOST PRECIOUS ASSET in my life…

NEVER will my love, respect, and adoration be less for you…

You are my RICHEST ASSET in MY LIFE…

I am ETERNALLY GRATEFUL for your "yes" in our wedded vows…

I hope we live to the century mark—still active, loving, and enjoying EACH OTHER. Thank "you" for Dinner and your love…

Your devoted Husband and *still* your love, John

Less than a few months had passed. It was a standout 2001. Madre was eager to compose JJ's letter on a picturesque card, the Pine Cove artistry of Thomas Kinkade. She was enthused by this "painter of light," spawning her art endeavors with a Kinkade golden-light style. The MMK (a.k.a. Margaret Morgan Karr) signature was advancing during these community-senior classes and novel endeavors…

My eldest sister, Patti Jo and I featured this light-filled art in our cozy homes. My landscape, oil painting became the last, revered art that Madre completed at 83 years young. Arthritic hands compromised a desired capacity for oil painting, but she never abandoned a joyful sentiment for divergent artists and galleries…

Now? I was equally euphoric, transported to seventh heaven and cloud nine. I witnessed her landscapes, portraits, still-life creations, and varied techniques on a daily basis in every room of my cozy condo. Madre's soothing landscapes, challenging portraits, and divergent techniques became an empowering gift for today and all measure of time…

I boosted my writing forte—electing the critical Madre letters for rereading. I was grateful again—that my historic, PJ cup runneth over…

You know that you are a young 68—so enjoy! You choose a nice dinner place to celebrate your day, John…

The girls will have you for a special trip, so you are blessed with a huge amount of love...

I know this one has been a hard year for you, as I developed more problems, but things should be better...

One day at a time—call it our time. Just fortunate to still be around and able to write...

I do love you deeply and we must look forward. Our needs are there for today and not the yesterdays...

We never walk alone because God gives us extra strength to try and tango on...

Thank you for all the strength you give me. You are my first Love and always will be in my heart, close to my very soul...

I do appreciate all your tasks around me daily and realize I have lost my independence—hard to cope at times, but we'll manage...

Wish I could make you a party like old days... Forever, your wife

Two years passed, but not the "Karr" tradition. Today became another fast forward to 2003. Madre penned her thoughts on beatitudes, prosperity, and paradise for JJ's special day...

I never knew how much my parents wrote about my health challenges and "PJ's tango on" attitude. With Madre's "paying forward" of the manila-clasped folders and diversified letters, I was privy to an inescapable, beautiful authenticity...

Happiness is something you decide on ahead of time. It is a decision that I make every a.m. when I wake up...

I have a choice—I can stay in bed and recount the difficulty I have with parts of the body that no longer work the way I desire. Or *get out of bed* and be thankful for the ones that *do work*...

Each day is a gift. I'll focus on the new day and all my happy memories I've stored away—just for this time in my life...

PJ *really* helped this year by doing so many family pictures to treasure—a very warm and thoughtful gift...

Old age is like a bank account. You withdraw from what you put in, so I deposit a lot of happiness in my bank account of *memories*. Thank you for filling my memory bank. God bless you for being YOU…

I love you so much! I have inner strengths like YOU to survive. I know that you have many days with back pain…

We shall do what our youngest PJ does—Tango on. Meet each day with a smile…

As a pair, we were meant for one another. Our whole, cozy home and pictures say that without a lot of words… Yours, forever

Madre lauded the familiar, rare feelings that both of them experienced from the beginning days of their romantic saga. Beliefs of complete love and endurance—mystical or known—were illuminated in her 2004 reflections…

You are truly the only man in my life and always *shall be.* Thank you again and again for marrying me and making my life *so complete*…

Somehow, God is letting us have one another…

It must be that our good life has made us endure all the struggles, because you had them. I, too, have endured…

Your strong, positive words keep me going. Again, we shall "tango on" like our youngest daughter, PJ…

Even though you call me "Boss," I have to be—so we can have better meals, eh? Enjoy your cake with all of our caring children…

Be sure to blow out your candles—89 years young! Hope you like your new shoes from your spouse and loving daughters.

Yours forever <u>and</u> ever, Marge

Rarified and mystical gifts...
Endurance and positive strokes of genius...
Defining moments and caregiving, a new
harmony and our mindful empathy...

It was 2008. Once again, I gave credence to that ardent phrase of Carpe Diem—Seize the moment. My PJ style of soul-filled writing arrived with a boldness, an impassioned bravado. I wanted to release the harmony, the rapture, and my bona fide sentiments—for Madre's birthday letter...

Madre— Famous women shared boldly about matters of the heart. Eleanor Roosevelt proclaimed, "You must do the thing you think you cannot do." Erica Jong, an American writer added, "And the trouble is, if you don't risk anything, you risk even more."

Eleanor and Erica offered their truths—*our truths, Madre*...

In matters of the heart, I believe ordinary women are also extraordinary. On your birthday, I celebrate *extraordinary* Madre—playful, beautiful, and soulful... Beyond our birthday gifts, it is providence and seemingly *divine intervention* that both of us share the real riches...

Playful Madre, even in the nursing home—as I gently unbuckle your sandals, take off your favorite Dartmouth "Big D" socks...

I fling one sock onto your chest and another towards your neck, a wee bit close to your glasses. Whoops! Dad and I chuckle heartily...

Eyes rolling, head shaking, and a Cheshire smile. Oh yah, that's definitely my *playful* Madre...

Later that day, I was ready to head home from Madre's nursing home. We did our thang (sic)—rubbing noses, a mother-daughter hug, and the melodramatic, airborne smooches tossed back and forth from the door to her comfy chair. My animated style and PJ antics brought forth her smiles...

Our dialogues and fun playtime typified my lively, whimsical Madre, even in her 90s. My PJ letter continued the memory lane...

Beautiful Madre...At 92 years young, I marveled and touched—your beautiful skin, your lush and natural hair. "You look beautiful!" A childhood flashback like, "Can you believe my mother and Dad are *that old*?" became my childhood allure (obsession!), given your "much younger" appearance. As an adult-child, I still exclaim, "Can you *believe* my Mom is 92? She doesn't even look her age…"

Our memorable times are sprinkled like a zesty seasoning—throughout childhood, adolescence, and adulthood. At each stage, the recollections delight! Madre on my "red snow wing" whizzing down our hillside; Madre as our perceptive, caring Girl Scout leader; Madre as the staunch supporter of my sports and leisure activities; Madre as comforter during my moments of teen angst; Madre as nurturer of my young woman's spirit; and Madre as the authentic supporter of PJ's evolving spirit…

Exquisite recollections of a remarkable, extraordinary Madre are PJ truths—OUR truths and cherished riches…

Always love and light, PJ (a supah! big Madre-PJ smiley face for YOU)

Anniversary and Birthday Letters
A No-Coincidence
Immersion of Sisterhood

Extraordinary! I came across an exclusive medley of anniversary and birthday letters in another manila-clasped folder. As I began to peruse, I became wrapped up in the no-coincidence phenomenon. They were primarily letters that my eldest sister, Patti Jo, had penned to Madre and JJ.

Remarkable! This no-coincidence immersion advanced with letters that I had scribed to Madre and JJ. How beguiling to come across only these letters of "eldest and youngest daughters" in the same folder...

As the last-born child, I began my composting—PJ letters and sweet anecdotes at earlier stages of development. Fast forward with this particular folder. The propagating and pollinating had matured and ripened since my early developmental years. This 1990 anniversary letter cropped up, coming from my composting garden...

By this time, my fruitful reflections were affected profoundly by the professional pursuits of nearly two decades. My flowering, looming PJ persona was generated from a top-shelf mulch...

An amazing cultivation—of grace and symmetry? Undeniably, I inherited the lifetime seedlings and nurturance from my unconventional parents. Other rarefied offerings? Illumination brighter than sunshine and a cosmic, royal bounty from parental care—all teeming from Madre and JJ's natural habitat. I was ever so thankful for our lofty garden of activation and incitement...

Happy Anniversary, Madre and JJ: As the years evolve, bringing a deeper understanding and appreciation for all that both of you have done (continue to do), I reflect and give "special" thanks. Perhaps, it is my profession of teaching-writing and a growing awareness of diverse cultures. Perhaps, it is an uncanny sense of intrinsic desire to shine a more radiant light upon my life experiences…

Whatever the unique process of understanding, I affirm and give that reflective time a top priority in my week. Even in my adolescence, I knew. I would partake of the intangible riches that others seemed to be searching for, yearning for…

~~I give a hearty thanks for the integrity and fairness with which you have afforded to *each* of your children. Patti, Beej, and myself have tried to engage fairly in our adult lives—at work, play, relationships, and more…

~~I reflect upon our values, a myriad of common bonds and values, and the individuality that emerged. There is no "one way" for all, thank heavens. It has made our bonds more genuine, our differences more appreciated. From that, each of us has learned *more tolerance* in this global world of ours…

~~ A very grateful thanks for modeling a sense of humor that has kept (still keeps) life in perspective—a true balance with our serious attributes and values. My students, friends, and hubby appreciate a "different" PJ, a heartfelt goofus who remains close to their heart and soul…

As much as I *really like* my own PJ attributes, talents, and weirdness (sic), I cannot say that I would feel this way with another upbringing, especially if it was one where my parents paid little attention to the intangible riches in daily living…

Your subtlety, space for growth, regard for our beings, and guidelines along the journeys (still going) are valued—more than both of you will ever know…

Always love and lasting friendship to the special, one and only…Madre and JJ!

My eldest sister, amiable and genial Patti Jo, was also composing and fashioning the alluring letters found in this particular folder. For this Spellbound memoir, even the PJ and Patti Jo letters with candid passages were written with "the three dots." I wanted to insure that Madre's perceptive foreshadowing about my Spellbound writings and her loving-kind gifting had a semblance of privacy— just like the beautiful letters of Madre and JJ in any of the prior chapters…

I fathomed that different readers would capture the core of sentiments, character, intimacy, and values. The PJ intention was to empower and sanction the readers' imaginative, intuitive, and savvy talents of discerning…

The common thread or themes depicted in the separate, private letters revealed the virtue and dynamism of harmony. Connections were an authentic part of this family memoir. I shall never forget or ignore—exactly how Madre nudged me in glorious, elevated ways…

There was a riveting life force—Madre's lofty vibrations with her encouragements noted in my Acknowledgments. "PJ, you know what to write…you have published for years… You will know what to share with today's world in need of love…"

There was a classic delight while scanning my 1994 letter. I had penned purposefully—with an abundance of comical acumen regarding our familial joys and my whimsical remembrances…

Remember when your "royal" nostrils flared and one, amazing eyebrow shot upwards? What a sight! The nonverbal cues reminded me of how important it is in a person's lifetime to take a stand—be firm, even courageous on certain days…

Remember when you posed with your beloved JJ for those romantic camera shots? My photo albums reveal the loving nature of your relationship, always so natural…

Remember when I visited from Texas to have my "New England" fix? Again, JJ and you infused the value of "our roots" and a sense of "time, place, and moments" which continued to arouse and renew all of my senses. You owned a parental pride, a loving resurgence of times gone by, yet not…

Remember when you visited the "great state" of Texas? I wonder where I inherited that love of travel and exploration? Hee, hee…

I met you in Galveston and Houston. Later, we traveled to the Panhandle, excursions around north Texas and then—into New Mexico…

It is your Spirit that keeps me going to new places and acquiring a broader world view of people, cultures, and attitudes…

Remember how we "look alike" after all these years? Finally, Madre! Yet, you know I liked that other people often assumed that I was Native American. Hey, I was along for the ride with our family outings, bronze-tanned and braided hair galore…

I am proud that I retain a semblance of Madre's blue-blood, royal genes. I *know* your life puzzle is the unknown background of your father, in spite of searches and hush-hush, blue-blood wealth, and upscale town records in that era. BUT—I claim that outer *and* inner beauty, especially from my blue-blood, regal Madre…

In my daily teachings, I know that the biological and psychological traits come from nature and nurture. As I teach, there is an elevation due to your unselfish ways. Madre, it is your precious gift to me—unconditional love… Always, smiling and remembering…

Unclasping another manila folder, I reached for a letter. It was part of the treasure trove for Madre and JJ's Anniversaries. I recalled that my oldest sister telephoned to convey her pondering about this 1995 letter. Patti Jo recounted that she had been feeling an uncanny momentum to write about her son...

My nephew was like my younger brother as we grew up. I would profess, "Hey, little bro'..." throughout our conversations or playtime. He never called me Aunt PJ (still doesn't). Awesome—we even looked like brother and sister...

In the office at my university, I hung up amusing, familial pictures and collages for the highfalutin' New England tales. Colleagues and students agreed that this nephew truly looked like my little bro'...

I went back to the musings of my eldest sister who died unexpectedly in 2005. That day's rereading brought a calm, an unanticipated quietude. I still missed Patti Jo, so I coveted my inner peace and the sanctuary that day...

...thank you for being an inspiration to each of us. Thank you especially for being an inspiration to my only child—my son—to attain a goal. When he needed it, you were both there for him to see what marriage can and should be. Bless you...

Today, I see the results of that unfolding, as he tries 100% to make his marriage work...

That's all that counts—the trying—win or lose, at least he tries...

I give credit to both of you, especially Dad's advice: throw out the stars *and* climb the ladder...

The effort is what counts—pick yourself up and go on...

See the flow from generation to generation. Thank you, Dad...

You Mom, deserve the thanks for your warmth, love, and giving. Let's enjoy that anniversary dinner to the max. You both deserve it, as parents and grandparents...

Thank you for honoring your responsibilities with love and concern over all the years—and more love to come...

You are the greatest! Words can't state how great. Your eldest poet is at a loss...

One year later, she was no longer at a loss of words, her authentic rhetoric. Patti Jo was able to express the uncommon beauty. Perhaps, her truism came forth readily because I lived far away for a long time and phone calls became our best-ever communiques. Somehow, I grasped the depth of our mystique. The intimate offerings would have happened, given the strong, sisterly bonds—despite our 10-year age difference...

I cherished that my heart-etched feelings were spot on. Patti Jo kept me spellbound and enthralled, rereading her joyful certainties...

I can say—thank you for your love as parents, for all you imparted to me while growing up...

Thank you for the strong foundation to build upon, when I could *not* do it as a child...

Also for guidance through teens, for prayerful standing by when I *rebelled* against it all, trying to find my way...

You were there smiling for me on the other side with parental love...

Your love as parents bonded all of us. Not many are so fortunate and blessed...

Have a special Anniversary memory. Dance a special waltz as love shines 'round *and* in you...

A year later in 1996, I was writing to my parents on an exceptional day. What rhapsody to be at our cozy, barn-red homestead for their 58th Anniversary! I had flown home for THE Eureka— to surprise my parents and to witness "the lovebirds" on their esteemed day...

What bliss, mirth, and rapture this amazing reunion engendered. Our storytelling? The tales were inevitable and irresistible. I reminisced and acted out the youthful actions...

JJ's drama-princesses—three daughters—strutted like peacocks to the maple table, sporting the posh outfits and costume bejewels. We were fixated on Dad's prancing around...

He would whisk out each chair theatrically and recite his poetic gems for each daughter. Yah, the feisty children in his life morphed into the feisty women. I took charge of the creative dramatics and stories at this 58th celebration...

The bewitching, magical images were recaptured with as much glee as my childhood antics. These exalted feelings and memories arrived on time—thanks to my airborne jet that zoomed from Texas to their 58th New England festivities...

Fast forward... As I matured, I pinpointed the uncommon touchstones. He was a Dad who chose to nurture his daughters and wife in spite of different norms for masculinity. He opened unprecedented doors to independent thinking and choices. He was a Dad who welcomed the individuality of women. He shared influential imprints of how, when, and where to offer our humanitarian efforts. How I cherished our JJ's perfect imperfections—then and now! I reread my letter, releasing the PJ head-nods and heart-vibes...

Dear JJ— I am writing to you about the beauty of times gone by, yet not...

The beauty of Madre remains vivid, no matter what she wore that Anniversary eve, for her love radiated throughout the room, as did her outfit and jewelry. I watched and watched...

How romantic—Mom and Dad dancing, smooching, and loving vibrations everywhere! Funny, how you remember the love and warmth felt in the room for all of us, but also that we saw the *natural, real love* between parents...

Plus the Anniversary pictures—so natural—revealed the tender love endured. As a young child and an adolescent, I knew those intangible riches were important...

Even in my early 40's, the images remained vibrant—in my mind, heart, and soul...

I *know* I shall always reach for those relationships which exude love and caring...

After all, I had role models and still do. That's the best...

How do you thank parents for that lifelong learning and giving, the ultimate "gems" in life? I think you keep *showing* how those values live on… I *always* will be so grateful…

It was still 1996, representing a prestigious 80th birthday for Madre. By this time, each of her daughters had pursued teaching at Sunday school, public school, and the university. Passions for the art of teaching catapulted us—stretch, discover, and appreciate a world— full of differences…

Each of us treasured our quality time with Madre. We engaged effortlessly in writing our narratives and prose, especially for Madre's 80th birthday. I chose my theme intentionally—the remnants of my lifetime lessons…

…Life passes by quickly, as if it is one big blur. And then? It appears to creep along slowly. You taught us. "Take *time* to smell the flowers. Smell the coffee…"

Madre, you shared the value *and* rarity of these phrases…

The longer I teach across the decades, the more diverse learners I get to witness, teach, and reflect about—even from a distance…

I often think of Madre! I cannot recall a moment, week, or year when you were *not nurturing or giving.* You *still* give of yourself to other people…

Madre is front and center—of our homestead….

You give abundance, sustenance, and life…

Without your love, none of your daughters could have dared to dream—all of our far-fetched dreams and reached for our lofty goals. Or, even attempted the undulating paths along our limitless, free spirit journeys…

God blessed your daughters—gave us YOU—beloved, inspirational Madre…

By 1997, there was a backbone of strength. A characteristic momentum over the decades gave rise to our robust energy, a magnificent verve. Such generosity of spirit and moxie were not only recognized but also adopted immediately by each of us...

We were now the adult children, the gratified daughters of Madre and JJ. It was no coincidence that our emotional learning curves came forth naturally. My older sister and I were acknowledging that we were on the same wave length with our themes of vitality and courage...

Today, although cold and wintry, shines warm with your love for each other and our family...

Your love for each other *and* us has given us a secure haven in a sometimes troubling world...

I feel blessed, as do all the family around you, to share in your happiness and an extension of that spirit to us. Your special Anniversary day shines bright...

May God's promises be new each day and evening...

Thank you for always being there—you're the greatest parents. Always love

I penned a brief Anniversary note to my parents regarding the multi-faceted layers and bonds in our family history. I highlighted that similar connections seemed to be lacking or sporadic, especially in times and places when the opportune chances for dialogue might have emerged in families. No judgements, just observations...

I paused to endorse and uphold an unvarnished truth. I was fortunate to be born into our family, regardless of the mutual desires and predispositions to own courageous dialogues...

I always remember your anniversary *vividly*—from childhood to now...

The shared times—us youngsters "dressing up" Madre-style, special dinners, and anniversary letters, BUT, especially our bonds and genuine love over those years...

Those intangible riches are a gift that no child, teen, or adult can demand or even imagine the worth—they are real or not...

I am so lucky to have you as my parents and special friends on *your day* and forever, close to my heart and soul. Mucho love!

In 1997, the abundance of my eldest sister's poetic voice imbued Madre's birthday letter. Patti Jo had been sharing her diverse prose throughout my years in Texas. This year I was lavished, showered with the tone of her messages and poetic voice. Patti Jo captured a universal abundance that she entrusted...

...May your year shine brighter than all the candles you've ever blown out. Thank you for always being by my side, for teaching me to live and love—by example....

You were teaching me to learn about myself by letting me grow. You gave to me a seed of your own being, nurtured with wisdom and watered with love...

Mother is so fruitful

as you blossom about

Your love so precious

as its spring fully sprouts

You guided from birth to

my own motherhood

You shield us when you should

and love us each step of the way

Mom, I'll always cherish

through each day of the year

May God, with all his saving power

Bless you with peace, so sheer. I love you always

A 1998 birthday note proclaimed a love of the progressive celebrations. As we aged, my oldest sister and I commented that our birthdays were becoming progressive. They became intriguing and fun entertainment with the lead-up and aftermath scenarios...

Thank you for all your love on my birthday—dinner, gifts, and special pie! January 1-7th was a great, progressive time...

The best part was all the love from family and having PJ here! We got hats in Boston. Later, we did our funny skits. Our hat "performance time" was the funniest…

You've sure got a group, Dad—now on film, creating legends! Traditions live on from birthday to birthday with the Karr's playtime…

As daughters, we fancied the charmed diversions and inherited traditions—literally! Our letters, whether birthday or anniversary, featured the melodramas and declared a relishing of the retakes—the TOTAL SHINDIG! Yes, we unearthed and spotlighted that ole' phrase…

Happy Birthday, Madre! What a fantastic 1998 year for you—60th wedding anniversary, 60th college reunion, seeing a granddaughter graduate from college, and more happiness to come…

Thank you for being the wonderful, compassionate mother you are—for teaching the love of books and to read *so young*…

Thank you for showing the love of family and how to keep the bonds so strong…

Your teaching of faith and prayer was the strong foundation for traveling through life and for teaching us to give and love…

Thank you most of all for being more than a mother—a *special* friend!

"Special Friend, Mom" (again, Patti Jo's prose was shared)

Friends are something

You keep through the years

Through the laughter

Through the tears.

A friend is someone

You lean on, too

You've leaned on me

I've leaned on you.

I'll always remember

the times we've had

Some of them good and the bad

Our time together is like

a song that comes to an end

But our song has a chorus

you sing again and again

God keeps you safe, giving you happiness and memories this year. Love always

This year was a cornucopian one with impressive imagery for Madre and JJ. Their 1998 travels across the United States and the "must-do pit stops" in various states rebounded...

My parents wrote, "PJ, you are the daughter that we travel to see. Your sisters live close to us, but you are far away. We get to take in the scenes and ventures on the way and returning home—feats that we never would have experienced. You always keep us guessing and wondering where you will journey..."

This birthday letter was conceived for JJ during their spectacular weeks in Texas! My parents aimed to enjoy the spontaneous travel. Finally, they arrived with the tall tales. The drama did not cease...

Their extended, six-week stay in Texas was brimming with a spontaneity, the hilarious sagas, and the never-forgotten imagery. Madre chose to type our stories, the awesome mini-memoir. JJ inserted his "gotcha photos" for the special TEXAS scrapbooks...

I tuned in intermittently—to the parental keepsakes in the TEXAS scrapbooks. What retrospective joys! I could succumb to the grand photos, a mini-memoir, and unmistakable caring, just like it was yesterday...

Happy Birthday—while you're in Texas! How sweet it is to have my Dad—dear JJ *and* special friend—in our homestead. As time moves along, I keep many memories closer to my heart and soul. I always feel your presence...

My childhood days in Ludlow are recaptured in your birthday letter. I recollect trying to make you mind with our walks when you wore a back brace after ruptured disc surgery. Even at my young age of 3 years—*what a NICE pain in the ass I was...*

Our visits to "Red" Jensen, bedridden yet full of a rejuvenating spirit, taught me powerful lessons—about life and *really living,* even in my elementary years…

Oh yes, we must not forget the bank visits where "my pennies were safe!" To this day, I can save monies. I have mastered an investment portfolio with annuity and diversity that reps "can't believe for one so young…"

During elementary and high school years in Natick, there were invaluable riches…

I watched my bright, innovative Dad go from helping Grandpa and Nana so long to *risking* a lot with a grandiose move and executive job in Bean Town. Your three companies thereafter opened the doors to the PJ *lifetime* lessons…

I knew more about the "real" world of work, politics, human nature, and teamwork versus the egocentric bosses, all because JJ stopped and took quality time to share the possible "why's"…

I have often thought that I was more successful with my jobs because I learned the necessities to survive *and* grow from you. I know without a doubt—I learned more than most women ever learned from their Dads—business-wise, socially, character-wise, emotionally, *and* spiritually…

So, how do you say thank you to *your Dad* for such gifts? I can't begin to place a value on the entirety. I shall know *forever*—these gifts are priceless…

Even as a younger woman with beaus and no doubt scaring you to death with some boyfriends, you let the reigns loosen. I could learn, beautiful or painful lessons, of the human spirit…

"Our home, like a bay or port, is always open. Readjust, stay, and then go back to sea…" Our home port allowed the avenues—to learn my vulnerabilities <u>and</u> strengths, how to nurture myself and an independence…

It is that independence—in my profession, marriage, friendships, family—that has let the "true PJ" shine forth…

Although my individual stamp of PJ is there, there is a unique blend of JJ and Madre within the core of my being—always! I proudly carry all…

I feel rich beyond belief. As I press forth with health concerns, no matter where they run their course, I can "dig deep" for that resilience and determination…

Life has an ebb and flow, humps and bumps, joys, love, and no guarantees. But, one can take hold of inner drive, spirit, and go forth, go forth, go forth…

With your spirit-filled vibes touching my heart and soul, I'll *survive* my difficult health scenarios and *discover* new accommodations. Your words, letters, talks, and love have rejuvenated me for years—as they do now through this long illness…

Your presence in Texas lives for eternity. Love to you—my Dad, JJ, and *best friend forever*…

The splendor of 1998 was destined to expand. My older sister heralded her own cornucopia of riches. Patti Jo would send her creative prose or excerpts in letters to my homes in Ohio and Texas…

In Under His Wings, her first chapbook of prose, Patti Jo included a sweet commentary. She professed her gratitude for my professional guidance and sisterly support. I was touched—rereading Patti Jo's perpetual gift of sensitivity…

Little did I know what the future would manifest. I paused to recapture our eldest-youngest, sisterhood chronicles. My sister and amazing grace—Patti Jo—died unexpectedly of pancreatic cancer on July 30, 2005…

I was stirred again in this exact moment of composition. Patti Jo left a different legacy before her ethereal journey…

Each year, an impassioned memory of Patti Jo swathed and draped my being. She died only five days after JJ's birthday—July 25th. She harbored and preserved our family legacy of love. That beauty shined in her shared letter and prose entitled, "Legacy from Dad"…

On your special day, Dad, I wish you good health, lots of fun, and laughs for the year…

May you win Powerball and travel the world. Thank you for being a father who is always there

for us and making home a refuge to always find love…

Thank you for a place to come for memories of good times, a peaceful place to return any time…

Thank you for your firm hand, your heart of gold. Thank you for making our family a bond

of love that time can't sever. Thank you for a legacy of love…

Legacy From Dad

While it's true as we age with each passing day

Unaware, we hold the key to immortality

For the love we share with others

Lives on in them

To grow and deepen

To be cherished, returned, and given again

In endless, ever-widening circles

Like ripples from a stone cast into the water

God blesses you for starting our legacy of family legacy.

I soared with that legacy of 1998 letters. I was rereading a narrative that set in motion the reminder—PJ's valuing of altruistic caregiving and the unlimited, complete attachments…

My parents returned to Texas to help as compassionate caregivers. At another juncture in my PJ-healing process and accommodations, Madre revealed a JJ birthday letter…

I reread at a slower pace. Then I nodded to my gods and goddesses. Ah, gifted again—the mindful heart and soul of two, humanitarian parents…

To my Special Man! Thank you "mucho" for coming to Texas. It will be a warm birthday for our "PJ" to have Dad on his day! It is time for a visit to these kids before we sell our home…

After 2+ years, we know she can't fly up here (her health!) and in another year, maybe our health will not permit us another trip…

Our mutual interests will expand to find our next "cozy home." We've been blessed for years… We have a unique love of 60 years, accepting one another's faults and still being very much at peace with one another…

You are my "Prince" as you signed yourself in my birthday letter—and always shall be. I recall loving prose—love as the spiritual coupling of two souls, two hearts that beat as one… I love you deeply—until eternity…

On Madre's birthday celebration in 1998, I undertook my reflections—cast upon the always-ripening beauty of her motherhood. There was no abruptness or bewilderment. My letter manifested unequivocally—as a tribute to her authentic aspirations…

Madre's Birthday Tribute: Over the years, people asked, "Who is *Madre*?" I immediately seized the opportunity to respond. "She's my mother and we gave her that special name—so deserving of because of her love, giving, and spirit of life…"

Other friends asked for additional anecdotes. They already heard of Madre's "wild" side with Ophilia—her infamous, Model-T Ford—drivin' way too fast 'round corners with Billy Mac, JJ, and other allies. Or, the infamous "Charleston dances" with whacks to her tiny buttocks and ankles flyin' high. Or, her arched eyebrow and flaired nostrils for, "I mean it, girls!" Oh—as if any of her daughters needed an affirmation…

Friends yearned for the storytelling a la PJ style. So, I dramatized JJ's romantic sagas about falling in love with this beautiful woman…

"She's like a beautiful stallion, PJ. You never corral that horse, never abuse the spirit. And that's what I *still love* in my woman…"

My friends heard of her generous nature, subtle lessons rather than preaching, and strengths as a woman. Madre's trademark was a smiley face on my letters, cards, and notes. Those tales traveled from New England to Ohio and Texas…

The friends who visited, and still visit, attested to their feelings. They conveyed, "I was so lucky!" I agreed, but added something else. "Our family relationships took effort, even if the luster was there. I learned that lifetime lesson from my parents…"

My tales continued for my friends (a favorite, Madre). I went to "shut-in's" when my braces and surgery hurt horrifically! I learned to focus on the good parts of my life, not just the rough edges. Many days and weeks, I faced the challenges with vestibular-neurological, thyroid, and related relapses. I inhaled courage <u>and</u> climbed upward, exhaling the fears that accompanied the debilitating attacks. I kept pausing as I wrote this tribute letter….

Like my Madre, I have a resilient chord, a determined spirit, and sense of spirituality. I trust that some roads begin a new pathfinding on our journeys…

I look forward to the laughter and adventures in Texas this summer—the "PJ Rod" is ready for a spin or two—you know, on those paved and unpaved roads! Or those treatments (a Madre declaration), at the ice cream parlors or Catfish Haven with homemade pies…

Whatever we do, as always, shall be spirit-filled, treasured, and "sunshine" for our heart and soul. With pride, honor, and much love, I am glad *you* are my "Madre!" Really glad…

Enjoy your day and feel the positive "vibes" comin' your way! Love you mucho!

Fast forward to 2001. "Yank-Tex PJ" was traveling back home. My diehard commitment—to SEE my family at least three to four times a year. My parents became wayfarers to Texas before and during their retirement years, but my sisters could not afford the wanderlust phenomena as frequently…

My self-promises were bona fide and ardent—visit and extract the rapture and indulgence of quality time. I chose to work one-term or no summers at my university, use my semester reprieves, and overlap my New England conferences with the familial visits...

Pure love! My eldest sister and hubby Don were always volunteering. It did not matter what time of day or eve. I amassed their marvelous hugs and kisses at the airport. What a treat! Winter sojourns would include Patti Jo's birthdays and my parents' anniversaries...

Rereading my eldest sister's feelings created an upbeat tempo and another unfeigned gift. Namaste, Patti Jo...

Thanks for my gifts and special party. Having PJ here made it even greater. I'm blessed with such a loving family. Thank you both for all your love and hard work over the years to make a *real family* for us...

If I get accepted at the Art Colony between all of your gifts, I got my theater outfit darlin'—as PJ would say...

Isn't God good? Years ago at Aunt Mildred's, I watched and thought—someday, I'm going to go to that art colony. The stories and people fascinated me...

Now, I may be one of those fascinating, creative people for a child to see and dream of going...

Thanks for the creative ways you showed parental love on my celebration! Love ya'

Well, my eldest sister became one of those creative recipients! She added a postscript to this letter. She would bake Madre's pumpkin bread and other goodies for her Art Colony week...

Patti Jo was practicing in earnest—what I taught her about Jin Shin Jitsu. She voiced how it made a difference—being on-a-roll and flourishing. I was elated, proud, and let her know ASAP...

In phone conversations, she noted the highlights of Madre's letter. Given this opportune chance to reread, I stopped to absorb her jubilation and bliss with parental guidance, patience, and prayers...

Her letter was dated June 10, 2001. Little did I fathom or ever envision—I would have only a few years to commune, grin and howl, bear hug, and kick up my heels with my adventuresome sister, Patti Jo...

...thank you for being such a precious Mom who had the patience to teach me to read. Now, reading is my favorite hobby...

You taught me to pray—and now, it is my work serving Jesus as a prayer warrior...

The Bible says, "Teach your children well and even if they stray, they will return to the right path." You taught your children well...

It must be a joy to have that kind of peace as a parent!

Each of us—Madre's daughters—opted to unveil our literary talents, our exposes, and a tradition of birthday wishes. Another letter, inscribed on a card with an inviting ocean shoreline, focused on "God's gift" from mothers...

This scene reminds me of our connections to water over the years—Winnepesaukee, Haviland Pond, Look Out Park, Farm and Dug Pond, and our family favorite—Rockport...

Just like that water—you have always been there for me in the ebb and flow of our lives, intertwined with one another...

Time may pass, but it doesn't touch the strong docks built along the way...

I feel that God has put you in my life to be my friend as well as my mother in troubled or happy times. And that's the most a daughter can ask of her mother...

I wish for you—whatever you want your birthday to be...

May God grant all your wishes for the upcoming year! Love....

It was still 2001. Patti Jo and I had been conversing and lauding strong fathers—their positive and unmistakable influences, particularly with daughters. I praised the new research, publicizing the benefits of nurturing, attentive, and giving fathers. These young girls, maturing to womanhood, had the higher self-esteem, the successes, and a confidence. No great wonder—why JJ received well wishes for a blessed birthday—from his self-assured and self-sufficient, eldest daughter...

The past year, I reflected upon your many blessings. God blessed you in the sale of your house and brought you to a great retirement apartment...

You are blessed with a loving wife—not all men are. You have her with you—not all men do...

Mom made tremendous progress this year with *your* determination and help! She can walk around and do many things...

You are blessed with *three loving* and *confident* daughters to help you enjoy so many things. We love you and try our best, each in our *individual* way, to help...

Some Dads have many children, but nothing from them...

May your day be special, because you are *special*... Love always

This same year, my parents illustrated the expanding world of unconditional attachment and sentiments—with another grand heralding of New Year's eve. It was a sanguine celebration—Madre and JJ's 63-year memoir. I took a break to envision the heavenly, golden aura that enfolded Madre, JJ, and Patti Jo. With today's writings, I paused to bask in my eldest sister's letter with her lambent memories...

As the winds blow and the snow falls, you must own wonderful memories of 63 years ago...

May you bask in the glow of the warm, loving memories over those years...

Thank you for letting me share many of them, dressed up so special as a child. You were so giving to include your girls in the festivities. They are memories to laugh about and cherish...

The gift of "sharing as family" is the best. I am *blessed* to have you as parents. I know I tell you that each year...

Only the Lord stands above you in my life. What more does anyone need than the Lord Jesus and family in this life? No awards, degrees, or money can take the place...

May you be blessed with another beautiful year together, hand in hand, one loving day at a time. My love <u>and</u> prayers will be with both of you <u>each</u> day... Patti

Indeed, 2001 was etched in our hearts as a gala holiday, given our Christmas appreciation and testimonials. Interesting—I found a note to my Dad—in the same envelope as Patti Jo's letter of divine sanctions. Madre's spiritual being was also rising on this 2001 holiday occasion—to capture a tithe beyond measure...

We are blessed to have one another—always close to my heart. Your true love has shone like the brightness of an evening star in caring daily and constantly...

Please know—I do appreciate all you do for me daily, John...

I could not manage *alone* and am aware of my disability. You really have a lot of *patience*...

On the bright side, we *hang tough* day after day...

When we love each other, it shows. We are given *new life*—hearts are full of new strengths...

Merry Christmas and may we celebrate many more...

I did not question why. I found more 2001 holiday renewals in this folder. JJ's card featured a comical dog who was barking, "Don't Worry!" On the envelope, he printed in a bold, calligraphic style: My Loving Wife! Get Well. We have many plans of joyful expectations and renewing loving memories together...

The dynamic, rallying notes were inside JJ's card. They touched upon the no-coincidence signs of mutual goals—a lucky penny and their determined, mystical spirits. Both keepsakes raised the bar for a healthy lifespan and their rampant, thriving adventures...

YOUR LUCKY COIN! Found this penny lying lonesomely—seeking a friendly hand at the entrance to the card shop. Many glanced at it, but I reached out, *knowing* the card was meant for "You!" So, my understanding and friendly gestures are your Good Fortune Omen...

Your lucky coin is meant to treasure for a LONG, HEALTHY, Happy Life together—filled with more exciting and rich adventures...

…I KNOW "YOU" CAN DO IT! Your loving, caring husband *knows* you have the strength and guts to do it… Your loving partner to Eternity, John

Well, Madre and JJ did greet that good-fortune anniversary in 2002. Again, I did not question why. The preponderance of tidings in this folder harbored "the eldest and youngest" sister-letters…

Yes, I opened the last letter of three. My mother hailed the allure of these jubilee moments and riches. My parents, as individuals and significant partners, favored the wonder and elation of internal worth far beyond any material tokens…

May your day be beautiful with precious memories and the future shine like your love, John…

To know you are there for me in happiness and sadness has meant more—than all the wealth in the world…

The Lord has blessed me with love and comfort through you. With family love, we will all walk to victory…

Each year I realize how wonderful you are—more than the year before. Your kind and thoughtful heart brings joy to every life you touch…

God blesses you always for the special part you play in my life… You are dearly loved…

I was back to reading our "eldest and youngest sister" letters with a Cheshire-cat smile and feel-good chuckles. It was a top-draw and A-1 summer—July of 2002…

Our splendiferous, fun-loving Dad and our loyal, entrusted comrade was on the cusp. JJ was definitely primed to revel and frolic in the gaiety of this whoopee-July birthday…

No coincidence, an expanding world of sentiments...
Eldest and youngest sister lifelines and bonds...
Sanguine celebrations and parental
attachment, always in our hearts...

Our family gathering of playful souls and spontaneity invigo-rated his high-jinks spirit. In the quieter moments that day, our Dad let the sentimental tears stream gently down his cheeks—as he reread another warm-hearted birthday letter...

May you have more great years <u>and</u> happy memories…

Thanks for being a wonderful father <u>and</u> good friend, one that I can turn to for advice…

You have strength to be drawn upon during times of trouble. You own the gifts of wit and fun…

You opened all of our lives to adventure and laughter, taught us to live each day to the fullest, and instilled in us life's greatest asset—family love…

Today, I wish you—sunny days that shine, a cup that runneth over with the best each day, showers from heaven to bless you, and lucky, four-leaf clovers strewn along your journey…

It was one month earlier, yet it embodied another compelling time to acknowledge our kindred spirit. I had been fostering and nourish-ing my birthday reflections for Madre. I was dogged, forging ahead, and healing holistically with the PJ health challenges. Our preeminent year of 2002 was full of imposing challenges, facing the music, and ultimately, impeaching our fears...

I begin my birthday reflections with my "kindred spirit," Madre. Both of us have climbed, forging the valleys *and* peaks, remaining intertwined as allied spirits, especially as we keep the next mountaintops in view! No matter where I am or where I travel, I've held steadfast to ALL your letters with "PJ, keep the faith…"

Your special smiley face has bolstered my heart. I have remembered—your urges to look for the "silver lining" in any PJ clouds…

Alas—the positive, self-fulfilling prophecy completes each of my journeys in small or gran-diose ways. All of us are imperfect survivors, but we can elect to learn anew. We can be enlightened at the places or knowledge we never expected to find along those journeys…

My Unity affirmations for PJ were a spiritual gift. "As I meditate in a stillness, I envision myself bathed in the healing light of my highest source. I am worthy of the power of my light. I am healed. Namaste…"

My affirmations came on a Sunday when I needed them to resonate in my core being. They have never left my PJ spirit, dear Madre…

An inspiring, higher source and guardians continue to strengthen my innermost core and resilience across the days and weeks…

And so it is! As I approach 50 years young and you become a magnificent 86 years young, isn't it truly amazing that these valued lessons are Madre-PJ keepsakes and return full circle? Another author shared that inspiration as a "profound gift to yourself." I try to take quality time to inspire myself, hubby, family, friends, and students…

I find, like others, that one can own fewer regrets. Together, Madre and PJ gain new-found strengths and synergy from my motto—TANGO ON! I give to you. You give to me. The circadian rhythms continue…

I celebrate this "special day" as a tribute to you and our home of heart and soul. I depart again for Texas, knowing that I carry our home, unconditional love, and the gentle cadence of kindred spirit. Love you—my Madre, friend, and kindred spirit forever

In 2003, it was JJ's incredible 88th birthday. It was about three years since the onset of his progressive dementia. Too soon— the insidious, ensnaring world of Alzheimer's would mutate and revolutionize…

But, for a short time period, there were bestowals. JJ still knew PJ. He knew his "youngest daughter" who flew frequently from Texas to New England. PJ phone calls, letters, and photos along with intuitive, observant Madre and my sisters helped. They bolstered every possibility of meaningful rhythms and images—of the Dad-PJ memory lane…

JJ communicated on certain cognitive levels, responding to fragments of our complex, fast-paced world. My Dad entrusted family, close friends, and my presence—bear hugs, smiles, simple conversations, and our loving kindness—wherever we went on shorter jaunts with his cane or walker...

Attentive to a sixth sense of intuition, a bravura, the intrinsic nudges, and an attachment to my Dad, I set forth purposefully. I settled upon the composition of a PJ "tango on" letter for 2003...

I did not know exactly when and how. I knew the crooked, snaky paths and the foreshadowing. Our revered, father-daughter bond would alter with an ever-encroaching future of the vastly different and the emotional-spinning world of Alzheimer's...

Tango on to 126—you're leading the way, Daddy! From those muscle-bound, handsome photos of prep school days to JJ's resounding "YES!" to living a zesty life now. Know that I am in Texas, toasting and cheering YOU in my heart...

Onward to the next mountain tops! My heart and spirit soar high—our visits and dialogues... You have my enlarged, beautiful photo of Madre and JJ on a plaque and my prose to greet *each* day. Much like my beloved colleague, guru, and "Yoda" Howard, you have the guardian angels of family and yesteryears. What riches in life...

We still know how to pack in the adventures galore, the dialogues to treasure in this lifespan and into eternity, and nourishing the love...always! As you celebrate on your special day, look again to that plaque and count the blessings of true love for 65 years with Madre...

Count the precious moments and memories of your three daughters who dearly love you—a man of honor—my unique, endearing Dad...

Know that you deserve and own the universal wealth that others seek. Know that love enfolds you each day, not just your special day. I keep you in my spirit-filled thoughts. Always sense my loving presence, as I do yours. Go forth with the renewal of spirit and *more* living...

Peace, love, laughter, and our sense of play. Tango on, JJ!

It was a memorable year. I wrote Madre's birthday letter in 2004 using an appealing notepad with a calligraphy script of Dr. PJ K-K featured at the top...

My graduate students had placed the exquisite parchment in an enticing "Dr. PJ Goodie Bag" to be opened—only after their graduation ceremony and our stellar visits...

Madre admired the ingenuity and resourcefulness of my graduate students that she had met in my university classes. She was privy to Dr. PJ's humorous anecdotes and touching stories for decades. No great mystery as to why I favored and decided to write on this special parchment for her birthday...

All these years, you have encouraged me through the humps and bumps, joys, and to search for the silver lining in any clouds…

You nudged me, waited unconditionally as I travelled along my journeys. You said or wrote, "Keep the faith and love." It was ok to make mistakes, try again, start over, plug ONWARD…

You know, by words and actions, how to love unconditionally. I honor your parenting, especially in light of your struggles. At this stage in my life, with most warts and idiosyncrasies exposed, I cherish our bonds that entice dialogues…

You elected to be different from your past. Saint Bernard of Clairvaux eavesdropped at our homestead: "We find rest in those we love, and we provide a resting place in ourselves for those who love us." I own no doubts. Madre and JJ will be part of my inner core forever…

There is a spark of the divinity in each of us, more purpose than we can ever imagine or envision. I remain grateful for your appreciation of my "wild woman" and sparks that propel me to places, known and unknown. Only you could embrace that "different PJ," striking out every which way or bust…

Truly, you are an appreciator of my adventuresome spirit, stubborn streaks, and whatever. You may worry, but it represents genuine concern and caregiving…

Together, we know how to let things go and have them return full circle…

'Tis the spirit of "tango on" and the dance I envision when we meet again in heaven. What more could a daughter ask for? I honor and revere your womanhood, friendship, mothering, and unconditional love on your birthday—and, ALL the days of my lifespan…

There was a rah-rah moment in 2005. JJ had surpassed his Dad, Mom, brothers, and sisters on this day—his 90th birthday. BUT—Life is not fair. It was a cliche that arrived for all of us. The revelation signaled a significant caveat, an unknown rite of passage in our family trailblazing…

JJ's dementia "stages" were in the lead, racing towards the smoldering, cunning trails to severe Alzheimer's. Our herculean journey would advance, like it or not, for the next thirteen years…

JJ owned a minuscule capacity to acknowledge—the PJ kindred spirit. My PJ heart-speak never stopped. This new pathfinding meant composing only simple notes of devotion. Madre, who owned tremendous clarity and perception into her late 90s, was elated. I still yearned to pen the JJ birthday letters—of my adulation, the new-found humor, and my unbounded caring…

You are the "gallant fighter!" You love LIFE. Always "tango on" and know that each day is a touchstone, a precious gift…

May you let your spirit soar to 98, 126…

May you always dance to the special music in life…

May you always know that your daughter PJ is here to rejoice, celebrate, humor, and comfort you. Happy Birthday—90 and onward! Much love (PJ smiley face)

Adulation and honor of parental longevity and verve...
Gallant fighters, Madre and JJ, hang tough against the odds...
Daughters—counterbalancing and juggling the
undulations of the known and unknown...

The resplendent days still made an appearance, a wondrous counterbalancing act amidst the Alzheimer's undulations. I was enamored with the grandeur of 2005. Madre remained a young-at-heart mother on her 89th birthday! She was overjoyed with our dinner, the Dairy Queen sundaes, and our cozy celebration at her nursing home…

Madre's room displayed a treasure trove—her artistry of oil paintings and Dad's unique framing, the comforting family photos, and the ever-changing flowers and plants. The familial, maple bookcases encased my parents' cherished nonfiction, fiction, and prose collections. Her medley of chakees revealed the prized gifts across the decades…

My birthday letter was reread after my arrival from Texas. As always, Madre had saved my keepsake—in a manila-clasped folder…

Happy 89th Birthday, Madre!

Partake of <u>each</u> day, a new beginning. We'll enfold one another in hugs, oodles of love, talks, a progressive celebration, and new beginnings…

C…*Courage* to seize the moments and make them your own

S…*Strength* to believe in yourself and in that power

G…*Grace* to celebrate who you have become (and are becoming)

B…*Beauty*—always take time to enjoy

I thought this anonymous prose, along with my additions, were super for your letter. Each of us owns the free will to have the courage to seize the moments in life's ebb and flow. It is our choice, our free will…

Isn't it amazing, Madre, to receive such a precious, daily gift? The strengths that we know we have versus the strengths we gain when we rise to meet each day and begin to open new doors, perhaps where others have closed. The unknowns tend to hold intrigue or anxiousness at any age, depending on our attitude…

It becomes a celebration of who we have become, like your 89 earthling years. It is part of grace, gratefulness, and who we are becoming…

"Tango on" is a step-by-step commitment that we share as mother-daughter. The beauty—inner and outer—surrounds us. It is always found in the eyes of the beholder…

Keep your "eyes wide open" during your special day. Partake and savor the memory lane. 'Tis a pathway that you can follow again and again. The countdown is so close, like our heartfelt connections. Soon, we'll be together. Ah, sweet harmony. Love always!

P.S. Remember the "tango on" sin sisters (sic). I know those fun scenarios in Texas and New England will bring laughter to your heart!

Fast forward a couple of years—to 2007. There was a recognition and respect of authentic fathers. Elated feelings of worth far beyond any monetary value along with a respectful balance of individuality and common, loving roots were touted…

I really feel lucky to have a Dad like you. There are kids without Dads, uninterested Dads, and Dads who simply aren't around every day…

You always made time to hear us, listen to what we had to say, and give us that much-needed family time…

Our memories cannot be bought with gold or sold over the counter…

You are either there for your kids or you aren't…

I'm proud of our family—all very different, yet united with roots established a long time ago…

United. Just like the beautiful reflection of the sunset—varied, full of color and texture, yet smooth and calm with a foundation of love. Luv, hugs, and kisses

JJ would have my letter, but there was a quick, affectionate note upon my December arrival from Texas. I was also excited to announce that I would be able to stay for their 63rd Anniversary in January…

This note is hand-delivered via "Big Iron Jet" to New England. OPEN it!

Dearest JJ—You know we have a "date" for a special birthday present—your SAS shoes made in my beloved locale of San Antonio, Texas…

Maybe the snow stopped us on Saturday, BUT not next week! I am flying into Bean Town. Watch out—here are JJ and "Wild Woman, PJ" to shop at our Panza Shoes. Clear the way…

It was a season for the additional milestones. I welcomed these benchmarks, the simpatico vibrations felt in my mother-daughter relationship as well. Our rapport and the attributes of Madre's motherhood were trumpeted…

A Mother's love is irreplaceable and understated, the nurturing seed to survive in an often crazy world. If we don't have that love, we are always searching…

Celebrities, the rich—those who have known only material things—appear to have so much. In reality, they yearn for the stability of a mother's love…

Children learn how to be better people when mothers show them the way— teaching truth in character, never wavering…

Mothers teach laughter and joy—a joy of being together, enjoying each other's untamed spirit…

Mothers teach the value of beauty and how to reach deeply into other souls…

Each of us can dwell in peace. I appreciate you as my Madre—for all you've done, for the riches that cannot be bought. You are a kindred spirit, my friend, and I love you for being who you are!

In my early 50s, I promoted and dignified a human capacity to become. I believed wholeheartedly—it was our choice, attitude, and altitude that would beget a sought-after stillness. The depths of this stillness could stimulate and nourish that becoming—a premier comfort and peace—for our mind, body, and spirit…

I wrote my Dad's letter, given this serene context of belief and despite the projection of Alzheimer's and its invasive detours. There

were times of vacancy, but there were moments of the unexplained,
unknown lucidity. Madre welcomed and saved my letters...

JJ, you are *young at heart* and headed for 126, as you continue the lifeline of the curious, inner child. You leave the doors wide open for the becoming of JJ. Thus, your remarkable attitude, tenacity to tango on, and *unconditional love* live on...

As your youngest daughter—a languishing, moonstruck PJ—I have watched closely from childhood to womanhood with respect, honor, and always, with a smile and tranquility. For me, you still mentor—those gentle nudges by Dad and what truly counts in daily living...

At 52, I am blessed, enriched, and bolstered forever with your ever-present, upbeat attitude, special JJ verve, and your playful delights...

You epitomize the written words of Albert Einstein. "Do not grow old no matter how long you live. Never cease to stand like curious children before the mystery into which we are born." My enduring, everlasting, and eternal Love

I was energized with this independent valuing—of choices, the
transitions, and lasting innovations. I carried out the PJ dreams and
aspirations, even when a "darkness" entered certain gateways in my
lifespan treks. A radiant "light" permitted my positive, honest, and
earnest journey, perhaps harder to find or begin on certain weeks...

I learned to search differently, liberate my free will, seize the day,
and pursue "the light" amidst any darker abyss. I opted for the remote
pathways and the art of boldness...

I was coming home again...

Happy 63rd Anniversary, Madre and JJ! Well, this year makes the second Christmas and Anniversary with both of you, my "special" parents and friends. I always hold you near and dear to my heart in Texas, as I share adventures with my own sweetheart...

After 20 years, we still dream about today and new tomorrows. I often wonder if we are blessed to enjoy 30, 40, 50, or 63 years together, like both of you. As your youngest, I feel privileged to have both of you alive…

The Jitsu, wild-woman PJ has arrived. Glad I was here through the surgery. Caregiving for one another is obvious, as our love and patience endure…

As Helen Keller wrote, "If we do not experience the darkness, we won't know the joys." So the *stumbles upward* have become my driving force, my motivation to go forward. I am defining the moments in the positive ways, professionally and personally…

The last 2 years, as I have journeyed back to my "port at sea," both of you have also experienced the *stumbles upward,* as we inspire and care for each other…

TEAMWORK goes a long way in one's lifespan and permits an intricate tapestry to be woven for each of us—no matter what age or stage of life. We have had wondrous visits, laughs far beyond what many people know in this world…

My hubby calls frequently to hear the stories and wishes he could be "cloned" to be in two places at once! You have embraced him as family, an adopted son. JJ has decided that his Dad's ruby ring be passed down to him as a "self-made man," quite a match to your Kipling's "If" prose that now resides on our living room wall…

Of course, he has mighty big shoes to fill with Grandpa and JJ. He loves that Madre said, "I'm so glad JJ gave the ring to him." Hope to return in March or May with a work conference. Meantime, I always feel your presence, wherever I am…

My students, new and old, know your beauty. So do my colleagues and friends…

I believe I am doing is what you instilled in me a long time ago—give back, give of yourself. There are many folks who are not born into such a family or they did not work at the bonds, even lost sight of the wealth in life…

In my profession, the PJ giving-back has opened unexpected doors and a personal zest for living. I have taken risks, enjoyed the plunge, and reaffirmed the "tango on" spirit with husband, family, and friends…

Giving back comes "full circle" when one lessens the self-pity parties or the self-absorption. Such a simple philosophy, but the drive to act upon that philosophy takes daily commitment. May the wind always be at your back and the light of my love remain in your innermost being, the core of life itself…

I was preoccupied and pondering a series of random thoughts and musings. A longing to pen the PJ reflections regarding our familial mainstays and unconditional regard kept popping up. Well, there was a terrific explanation. The time was three years later—a true-blue triumph and fortune—Madre and JJ's awesome 66th Anniversary…

As a growing tot and child, I brought home new friends, kindred soulmates, and, of course, the first yahoo-boyfriends. As always, you welcomed ALL…

You opened your hearts, creating room for charm, liveliness, dialogue, and the best give-away—our family delight of play…

As a youthful teen and young adult, I brought home playmates and "beaus" who were embarrassed or not as connected with their parents. I had my "teen" moments, but PJ's dragging-home-everyone syndrome reigned supremo…

Forever on a journey of becoming, I have kept my inner promise of "coming home," no matter where I lived…

My "coming home" begets the well-known and unanticipated pleasures. Unified moments and family images remain vibrant…

From "the yesterdays" to "the now," I am elevated in life. I carry a pride—who I have become and who I am becoming…

On your 66th, much love

Majestic interlude, the Cathedral of the Pines...

Symbolic rest, peace, and eminent signs...

Awakening light orbs in ascension, nodding

to the gods and goddesses...

What The World Needs Now
Love Sweet Love

Fast Forward—it was August 4, 2012. Visiting Madre at her nursing home, something began to stir in my heart. Suddenly, in a rousing moment, I was informed.

It was almost a year since JJ's death. There was a wall calendar and a pocket calendar in her end table, but I already felt a certainty. Madre never forgot the exact dates—JJ and Patti Jo's deaths and any signs of their ethereal journey...

She was 96, an admired elder at her nursing home. With today's visit, Madre was vivacious. Our kindred spirit and dialogues were incited and catapulted—by a sentimental tune and accompanying lyrics playing on my treasured iPhone. What the world needs now is love sweet love...

Madre spoke courageously. It was the quintessence of their love story, an oral rendition that she wanted me to hear and compose. She paused, making direct eye contact whenever I looked up from my scribbles in our defining moments...

By this point in my life's pilgrimage, Madre was cognizant and awaiting the next PJ writings, wherever and whenever...

Today was no exception. Madre's choice of words for the dynamics of their love chronicles was embodied in an obvious tenderness...

We *always* kissed each other good night, even if we had an angry spat. That was *rare* in all of our years of marriage...

Both of us transferred that love—our *real* love—to you as kids...

Simple things! Your Dad and I wrote with a simplicity in our birthday and anniversary letters to each other...

Unconditional love and our individuality were always there. That was the comfort *and* beauty...

Love made you peaceful. Even when we had bad times like the Depression, a lack of money, major health concerns, or issues with raising you kids (she stopped to be sure that I spotted that notorious Madre look—you know what I mean!)...

Love was *still there* in the tough times. Love sustained us. Love will sustain you, PJ...

Madre stopped briefly, but with a full intention—to dignify her childhood and adolescent lineage. She cherished her New Hampshire relatives and grandparents who truly raised her. Madre was aware of how much her grandmother was present, attentive, and "loved me so very much..."

Madre etched and refreshed the critical years that contributed positively to her morale, a confidence, and her womanhood. She was quick to attest and endorse her charming Aunt and Uncle who remained supportive during the early stages of my parents' marriage...

My Aunt and Uncle would show up in Nashua. I would get a perm, not a cheap one—a *good* perm for my hair...

I look back and wonder how we did it. During WWII, your Dad was gone four years. That was a *long* time...

During the war, there were letters more than phone calls. Too expensive...

Everything was in code—in his letters. I would know—he was ok. That was important…

I savored Madre's decisive pauses, her soul-filled eyes, and the colorful, sharp remembrance of JJ's attempts to humor her through-out the traumatic war years. He did not want her to worry so much. Madre began to chuckle softly…

One letter… Don't worry because I am in Hawaii. Just old women with droopy boobs hanging around. Nobody to be jealous of, Margaret…

Fast forward from the war years—to her animated memories of Ludlow in 2012. Madre was literally glowing with today's oral history. She was an eloquent storyteller of yesteryears and their "cozy homes and best neighbors" on Elm and Hubbard streets…

Ludlow was a small, mill town in western Massachusetts. Madre ended today's tales, praising a highly regarded doctor who died recently, but practiced well into his elder years. Dr. D— was our brilliant and empathic family doctor who still made house calls. No wonder the folks had a town statue made in his honor after his death…

Dr. D— The design was a stately, bronze statue. It was a prominent Ludlow Memorial…

He went to heaven for sure! Dr. D— made house calls, the *only doctor* that would spend that extra time…

Dr. D— didn't charge us much! He took care of the poor…

It was a few months later, November 8, 2012 to be exact. At 96.5 years young, there were still mesmerizing stories—Madre's oral history. Those riches transpired with my frequent visits to her nursing home…

I declared that Madre never needed to make a "bucket list" in her lifetime. She had managed to pursue what others would call their next dreamscapes…

Do the *right things* in the world. Try to do your *best*…

Do exercise. I still work with my ball for the arthritis in my hands. I walk the hallways in the nursing home with my walker. There's a nice sun room to sit and talk…

Attitude counts! I drove the car until 83, then osteoporosis prevented me from driving. Yet, I still rode with your Dad, reminding him of the short cuts <u>and</u> the beauty of our scenic roads…

Eat the right food, like fresh corn on the cob. On the farm, my Grandfather would tell my Grandmother to pick the corn right out of the garden *fresh* and cook it…

We would ride the wagon on our 200-acre farm and stop to pick our blueberries. You had to watch carefully for any mother bear and her cubs…

Forget jealousy. It is *not* worth it…

I am *kind* to everybody. Most people are *kind back to you,* particularly if you're in a walker…

Now, I have a wheelchair so I can go to more activities with you girls or the staff. I even went to your condo, PJ. I'll *always remember* PJ's cozy home and—*all* of my art work displayed…

Flashbacks happened whenever Madre was speaking about her wheelchair. One recollection was my abiding, deep-rooted imprint— from a stellar Grandparents' picnic at her nursing home…

Madre was eager to attend, but anxious due to her wheelchair. Only she could participate, as Dad was now in the severe Alzheimer's unit a few miles away…

No worries, Madre! All of us—PJ, Beej, Marty, and Antonio— alleviated any concerns, brought her outdoors in the wheelchair, and rallied at this Grandparents' gala picnic. Irresistible, charming Maurice was coming to play his accordion and encourage the sing-alongs…

They already knew. As Maurice approached our table, he knelt down beside Madre's wheelchair. One look, simultaneous nods with smiles, and then—their rendition of the song. "All of Me" was performed by this hyped-up duo. Of course, Madre and Maurice's musical debut was followed by hoots and applause from the crowd and each of us...

My eyes welled with dewy-eyed tears. It was my parents' favorite song, just shy of their soul-filled 74 years of marital swales and valleys, the pinnacles, and a rapture...

I was confident and held fast to my belief about positive vibrations from the world and universe. PJ could and would write forever. I heard those unforgettable echoes of Madre's words. Choice and free will accelerated my next decisions...

Write an epilogue with the eye-catching phrases in their letters across several decades. Be sure to include my PJ "witnessing" and the meaningful reflections. Write about the esteemed flashbacks—Madre and JJ's spirit and fortitude...

There were no disbeliefs, hesitancy, or skepticisms. Whatever themes had "popped out" in letters and diverse chapters would be a culminating, sublime closure for this Spellbound memoir ...

Epilogue

There was an unmistakable reappearance of eye-catching phrases. Stirring letters within the varied chapters capped a span of decades and a big-as-life attitude. There was a mystique and charismatic force, even though I knew Madre and JJ as my shepherding, light-filled parents and treasure friends.

I had owned the opportune "witnessing" of an incredible bonding between my parents for fifty-five plus years. And, for this book, the Spellbound memoir? I received and welcomed another guiding ray of incandescent light from Madre...

Madre reaffirmed a soft spot—the PJ adulation—for writing and my next book, noting how I could preserve their lifespan letters during times of struggles, dreams, and fulfillments. Just continue—another book and PJ's paying forward—their love sweet love that the world needed...

Madre continued this benevolent cache—their enthusiasm, the trials, and the tribulations—with an oral history during many visits to her nursing home. The awesome layers of caring invariably touched my mind, body, and spirit. Like a favorite melody, Madre replayed their lovebird, humorous, and upbeat stories...

Then and now—I elected to make the conscious choices. I became intoxicated with the pleasure of their words and phrases, whether spoken or written—a rarity for my parents' generation. What an honor to be in sync with these precious moments gone by, yet not...

I wanted my readers to open to any chapter, any of the letters, and just read. The messages and decades of unconditional love mattered. For a shorter legacy, I knew that I would compose this Epilogue in concert with Madre and JJ's definitive spirit and fortitude that stood out...

Madre and JJ reflected a dynamic-duo synchrony that was spoken and written during their meaningful decades of togetherness. Indeed, their individual spirit and fortitude encapsulated their epic love—for my family and the world...

Witnessing and Reflections
The Spirit and Fortitude of Madre

Souls echoing *and* growing forever fits us perfectly, John…

Our spirit and souls will always meet. Yours *forever*, Marge…

Depths of our souls—we experienced that *different* love from the very beginning…

An aside: My parents were close to the 74th anniversary when JJ died on September 3, 2011.

Their "All of Me" song still resonated… Both of us sang *our song*, John—All of me, why not take all of me…

Somehow, we made it through many hard times. We would march on to that drummer with a positive beat. John, you keep saying to me, "Think *positive!*"

When I look back and watch our daughters, I know I lost something growing up. But, *we* have quite a *family* now, John…

We value our individuality. We have a blend of independence. The *oneness of our love* will be the most convincing factor for our children…

Both of us experienced and appreciated nature way ahead of having any children—our Hanover moonlit nights, gazing at the stars, our dreams to travel to brighter stars and afar—*into the universe…*

John, we always expressed that we were *ahead* of our time…

We were wealthy in the right way. Just the *oneness of our love*—one in another….

We *trusted* our caring, understood its value across the decades. And, our lifetime faith of our love into eternity, John…

I feel so deeply for you, until my last breath and beyond. One day you may be the one to scatter my ashes to the winds and to let the flowers grow. Remember me with a kind deed or word to someone who loves you deeply, namely our three daughters. *Then—I will live forever in your heart and soul...*

The world has more need of gentle hearts and love that are warm, John. Your thoughtful deeds make the world a *better place* with your kindness...

You give strength and love without asking anything in return, a *rare benevolence* of inner quality that few possess...

So many families today do *not* have that bonding of love. Somehow, our strong love passed along to the next generations...

Always—your wife, lover, and friend. You are my *closest* friend and confidant, John...

We are blessed to have one another at this stage. I am *thankful every day* that we see the sunrise together. It is a peaceful *and* comforting feeling...

You wake me up every day. All we need is our great love to sustain us through struggles *and* happy moments—of which we have had many—*more* than we can count...

We have had so much *fun with so little,* darling...

Love you *completely,* John. I would like to shout it to the whole world. My unconditional love reaches way down into the *soul*...

You called me the "star" in your life. We've reached for all of them. Some we've captured in our happiness—and yes, in our struggles. *There are more stars out yonder for us to discover...*

Fast Forward. There were thirteen years of dementia, Alzheimer's, and the unexpected nose-dives. The roller-coaster effect became a metaphor for JJ's moderate to severe Alzheimer's life force. The PJ adrenalin-rushes left behind the unforgettable, bittersweet imprints...

My Dad—a sharp, vivacious, and responsive JJ of yesterdays—was transforming beyond anything I could ever project or imagine.

Juggling and shuffling my life, the bionic eyes upon my cell phone—even in bed, and seeking a readiness for the upcoming learning curves became the "new normal" in my life...

My PJ heart "ached" with JJ's spiraling changes throughout his backsliding and moderate stages. Then came the skids—his severe Alzheimer's downfalls...

My family memoir—Spellbound—was like a prism of reflections and refractions. Now, there was a stretching, far beyond the former chapters. Here and now, I was attempting to recapture and write JJ's authenticity—what I witnessed, what I overheard for a reason, and what I experienced during his thirteen-year evolution...

Our mother was still called *THE QUEEN*. JJ would look or stare, revealing his new, half-smile and would still let us into his space with greetings and hugs. But, he was quite anxious with the staff. He would blockade his door regularly with our family table and chairs...

Downsizing his room to a twin bed, dresser, and chair to stare at a television came too quickly. He was stashing paper towels, Kleenex, and different belongings from other residents in the locked dementia unit...

JJ was able to write—periodically. TO MY QUEEN—was *slowly printed* on the cards that my sister and I would bring to his Dementia unit...

JJ knew the moment that his daughters entered his downsized, spartan room. PJ and Beej would refill his locked, med kit and would help change the batteries for his old style, Analog hearing aids. He grew impatient as we scrambled to finish these must-do items for the staff...

"When are we going?" became JJ's relentless question. Or, there were his repetitive stories about people "stealing my things..."

At least JJ still knew that we were taking him out of the locked-and-coded door to go down the elevator. The door was outside the main door to his dementia unit and one floor from his QUEEN Madre...

JJ could still walk with us using his walker, given our repetitive cues and reminders. He still wanted to see and greet—HIS BRIDE…

JJ and Madre would accompany us to the beautiful, main dining hall—until he no longer could function in that exquisite setting…

I shall never forget the precious images—his pausing to talk to others—just a few kind words. JJ's blue-blue, twinkling eyes would slowly disappear across the next years…

Madre's eyes brimmed with tears, but she made a bold move. "I'll go to his Dementia unit for his family lunch…" She did. Madre took loving care of whoever else was at JJ's table…

JJ began to loose communication skills and become reticent, but would eventually respond to our gentle touch, quieter talks…

JJ's next declines meant new applications ASAP, the too-long waiting lists, and finally, an unexpected and amazing grace—to live in an exclusive Alzheimer's facility. It was only a few miles from his lifetime soulmate, Madre…

JJ's last home at this facility was a three-bed and male-only room on the top floor. All of the "severe patients" were the men and women whose world was labelled "severe Alzheimer's…" Beautiful, consistent caregivers—nurses and CNAs—changed his diapers, dispensed the meds, dressed him daily, and more…

JJ and our beloved Dad of yesterdays were waning fast. Yet, he was cognizant of my sister and I on *some level,* accepting hugs and kisses in his JJ space, this insidious world of severe Alzheimer's…

My cell phone was always ON, laying beside me as I slept—for good reason. Several hospital emergencies arrived. I zoomed—FLASHERS ON—to keep up with the ambulances…

Going into emergency rooms, I scurried alongside JJ, talking aloud to reassure. I still sense that inner hope for less paranoia and outbursts—in JJ's too frightening, outside world…

Choices, options, decisions—constant visits by my sister and myself plus a few visits by Madre who could only cope with our best photos and a short synopsis of our visits…

JJ perceived or somehow fathomed our kindred spirits, never the names of his daughters or wife. My sister and I lost count of our loving-kind visits—throughout JJ's mini-peaks and the countless quagmires of thirteen years…

JJ would lose his obscure, vacant eyes or the inevitable stares for nanoseconds. Then, he slipped back into a darker abyss—that none of us could decipher or imagine…

JJ's eyes would brighten with the rare Madre-visits. We brought him down to the ground floor that housed comfortable couches and chairs in a lovely lobby. JJ's hand clasped Madre's out-stretched, petite hands. She would relay their love stories, until JJ's vacancy and "unsettling anxiety" reappeared…

Up, up, and away—to the locked, top floor—his comfort zone *and* home now…

Madre came with my sister and myself when JJ was dying. His nursing staff and the foreshad-owing? JJ had only a few days and that weekend—or a month, perhaps…

Day by day—the three of us came to his bedside. Madre held JJ's hand, sharing an oral his-tory, their epic love story. My sister and I shared our tales, letting only our welling tears and gentle embraces come forth…

Each day, we left Madre with JJ for a private time. My sister and I hugged one another on a couch in the hallway. Only then—the vibration of our souls and quieter sobs were released…

Madre finally *released* JJ, disclosing that she would meet him—in eternity. That visit was Madre's last earthly witnessing—of her beloved John, Johnny, JJ…

The next day was our consummation and a swan song. Beej and PJ's last, earthly witnessing of our beloved Dad—witty, feisty, and loving-kind JJ…

Witnessing And Reflections
The Spirit and Fortitude of JJ

I am in indebted to that *unknown force of nature or God* which brought us together, Margaret…

The people in Margaret's orbit are *enriched* each day by her voice, look, touch, and love…

Yesterday, I did not know as a youth. But today, as I look back, you have made life rich in innumerable ways…

It takes a loving, knowing, and compassionate woman of great understanding, like you, to make him *truly a man* each step of the way…

Like a top chef, you have been that ingredient added to the "mix" which gave *the gift of life together* a new meaning…

The tango of life, together like the dance, how else could you describe our relationship? It is a story of passion from the day of our <u>first</u> dance together…

The twinkle and gleam the first day I SAW YOU. I knew you *and* I belonged together…

In tough times, you loved and inspired us to try and surmount the obstacles. As I daydream and look back at events, "you" have been the *driving force* in our successes…

Whatever mysterious forces drew us together and helped to solidify our love, they did not err. But, I must acknowledge and credit us for *working together* with understanding to build upon those good fortunes…

I am *deeply grateful* as I see others about us. We love too much to hold any grievance, a purposeful step taken to hold a richer treasure—our love…

I have stated many times that they destroyed the "mold"—that is why—there is only ONE of YOU…

We did it "our way" together! Floor the gas pedal *and* Let's Go…

Let it be said in the winds of time—they loved, worked, dreamt, and achieved with some small measure of accomplishment. Suddenly, it came to me—we could not have a better gift to each other—our trusting *and* deep love. It is greater than any material gains…

Every moment of life with you is an exciting adventure! I love it that way. You will hear *no regrets* on my part…

There is *my respect and honor* of you as a woman of intelligence and companionship. It takes a great partner to shape the future. I thank you in advance for the years ahead—together…

I called us a *miracle*, just as I have our felt our meeting years ago. That turned my life into a different pattern, a wonderful one over the years…

We can't sit still you know. It's our restless love and adventurous urges that make each anniversary the *"new beginning"* together, adding to *"our book"* of a long life together…

You are like a rare wine. You drink slowly, rolling over ALL the taste buds of life…

You are brave and determined, proving healing can be DONE with faith itself, the medical staff, and the good Lord or Spirit above…

Hope we are destined for the Century mark. I truly can say from the *innermost depths of my heart,* I look forward to that…

Hopefully, love is beyond the body life, into the *spirit world* of the unknown…

I am—*Your mate until Eternity…*

Namaste

~ ~I owned—a definitive confidence *and* deference to Mother Earth "Gaia" and the universe. Madre and JJ were now the soul-filled beings—no traces of the tough, physicality issues for Madre and no traces of the insidious, ensnaring world of Alzheimer's for JJ…

~ ~I owned—a certainty. Madre and JJ did become the forever-lovers into eternity that they expressed in generous, lofty letters across the decades. Perhaps, they became the "avatars" of their generation *and* my PJ manifestations as ethereal images or majestic orbs of light…

~ ~I accepted—the power of vibrations and a life force in today's books by renowned authors. Kinesiological testing of "critical consciousness levels" was an authentic phenomenon. Individuals who were at 300 to 700 levels resonated, counterbalancing the people who were below 200. They made a quality difference in our world countenance *and* our survival…

~ ~I pressed onward and upward—my PJ immersion with intriguing, contemporary books. There were credible affirmations of my beliefs—the "avatars," the "earth angels," and the metaphysical dimensions in our world and in the universe…

~ ~I entrusted—all of my "no coincidence" signs and imagery. The "witnessing" and telepathic messages came forth after Madre and JJ's deaths—and, in any defining moments thereafter. I made a conscious choice to remain attentive and honor—the known *and* the unknown…

In Loving Memory

In Loving Memory of
Margaret M. Karr
June 10, 1916 - June 28, 2013

Namaste, Madre, JJ, and Patti
Until we meet on the other side...